# AGAINST
## the
# CLOCK

## Other Books by the Author

*Let's Glorify God*
*Missions in Crisis*
*Prayer: Common Sense and the Bible*
*The Holy Spirit: Common Sense and the Bible*

# AGAINST the CLOCK

## The Story of Ray Buker, Sr., Olympic Runner and Missionary Statesman

by

### ERIC S. FIFE

ZONDERVAN PUBLISHING HOUSE
OF THE ZONDERVAN CORPORATION
GRAND RAPIDS, MICHIGAN 49506

**Library of Congress Cataloging in Publication Data**

Fife, Eric S.
    Against the clock.

        1. Buker, Raymond B., 1899-        2. Missionaries—China—
Biography. 3. Missionaries—Burma—Biography. 4. Missionaries—
United States—Biography. I. Title.

BV3427.B78F53        266'.613 [B]        81-7560
ISBN 0-310-24351-3                       AACR2

Designed and edited by Edward Viening

*Printed in the United States of America*

# CONTENTS

95529

# FOREWORD

Most of us live and die unnoticed, unapplauded, unsung. We may be appreciated, of course, by our families and friends, but once they too are gone the memory of who we were and what we did rapidly fades. As the psalmist comments, "A man's days are like grass, he blossoms like a flower in the field, the wind blows over him, and he is gone, and his home doesn't know him anymore." How, then, can we preserve and transmit to the generations who follow after us the inspiration and challenge which God through some of His gifted servants has permitted us to experience? An authentic biography is an obvious medium for conquering oblivion. I rejoice therefore to know that long after both Ray Buker and I have entered the Celestial City people will be blessed and influenced by him as they read Eric Fife's chronicle of my friend's pilgrimage.

Well-known indeed, yes, even hackneyed are these lines by Longfellow:

> Lives of great men all remind us
> We can make our lives sublime,
> And, departing, leave behind us
> Footprints on the sands of time.

Agreed. But what makes a man great? In my opinion (if I may speak in the past tense of a contemporary who, I am grateful to report, is still vibrantly alive) Ray Buker was great as a man of faith. From childhood on he knew, loved, and trusted the God of Abraham, Isaac, and Jacob, the God and Father of our Lord Jesus Christ. His was a deep, unwavering trust in the gospel. His was a childlike confidence in divine guidance and direction. A man of faith, he had the courage to venture into Burma and there with his family triumph over immense difficulties and dangers. And his faith was the source of his courage.

Ray Buker was great as a man of vision. A Yankee by birth and background, he was the antithesis of provincialism. The Bible gave him a planetary perspective and a global burden. It ignited in his soul a concern to reach lost humanity with saving Good News. It motivated his ministry as a missionary, a missionary executive, and finally as a professor of world mission in our own seminary.

Ray was great as a man of prayer. I know first-hand something of his systematic and diligent intercession. As a missionary executive, he was more than a prolific correspondent who wrote prodigiously to his colaborers overseas. He prayed for them as well, persistently day after day.

Ray was great as a man of discipline. His extraordinary energy and driving dynamic were channeled effectively by habit and routine. Aware that we are finite creatures, he worked as he had run against the clock in his early years, not frantically but with an unrelenting doggedness. So he had time for exercise, time for prayer, time for voluminous reading, time for vast correspondence, time for an amazing range of friendships, and always time to reach out a helping hand to his struggling fellow-pilgrims.

Thus in my opinion Ray Buker—cherished friend, longtime colleague, trusted confidant, kindred devoteé of Robert Browning, model of Christocentric living—was great preeminently as a man of God. Except for this biography and the precious memories of those lives he touched, his name may be submerged in the turbulent sweep of ongoing history. But what Luke says about John the Baptist I say sincerely about Ray Buker: he was "great before the Lord."

—*Vernon Grounds*

# ACKNOWLEDGMENTS

I am extremely grateful to Dr. Raymond Buker Sr. for many hours of interviews he gave me plus innumerable telephone conversations. He also placed at my disposal the massive family archives, including an account of the origins of the family, and the early life of the Buker twins compiled by Minola Buker (and typed by Mrs. Mary Margerum Buker). Mrs. Mary Buker has always been far more than a competent secretary—also a charming hostess during many visits to their home.

I learned much from interviews with Dr. Richard Buker, and also from Dr. Ray Buker Jr. The Athletics Director at Bates College put at my disposal many press cuttings dealing with part of Ray Buker's athletic career. Mrs. Ginny Viola spent many hours scrutinizing microfilm in Boston Library for accounts of the Olympic trials that appeared in the *Boston Globe.*

I am indebted to Dr. Vernon Grounds, of Denver Conservative Baptist Theological Seminary, who advised me on books to read. The librarian, Sarah Lyons, also gave me prompt and competent assistance.

Mr. Ed Viening, my editor at Zondervan, had his patience sorely tried by all too many delays—I am deeply grateful to him. Many people assisted me with their experiences in connection with Ray Buker. I believe all the names have been mentioned in the book, but if I have overlooked anyone I am deeply sorry.

Most of all, I deeply appreciate the unfailing help and patience of my wife Joan who has been involved in every step of the project.

# PROLOGUE

The light was dim even though it was early afternoon. The jungle of large trees was covered with thick vines that formed an arch overhead. Not much sunlight could filter through.

The trail was narrow, never more than three feet wide and often less. The ground was rough with tree roots and rocks, which made traveling treacherous. It was hot, too hot. Clothes clung to the body and streaks of sweat ran down the faces. Would the trail never end? The little party had followed it for days, and it seemed like an eternity.

The trail zigzagged in all directions. There was only one thing that never changed—it was always up, up. Would they survive? That was the crucial question.

This land was inhabited by bandits and headhunters. This was not the time of year that headhunters were a danger but the bandits were a different matter; they were always a threat. The leader of the party was armed but he knew that he would be outgunned if bandits attacked. However, he had learned to live with that threat.

It was a small group of people and ponies. The leader was a man who was as tough as nails. He was only 5'7'' and had close-cropped hair that needed little attention—ideal for these conditions. Years of travel such as this had forged his natural toughness to a fine edge. He was wearing rough native garments, a short tunic with baggy trousers. Few would have guessed that he had participated in nine years of competitive running culminating in an Olympic gold medal.

The trail became much steeper, and the leader asked the guide, "How much further?"

"*Acci muka,*" he replied mechanically, "just a little further." It was the same reply he had given all day.

The lives of the party depended on Ray and he knew it. He had survived his years in the jungle not only by being physically tough; his reflexes were lightning fast. They had saved his life on many occasions and would do so again. He relied not only on his stamina but also his head. His thinking was always alert to anticipate trouble ahead. His eyes gave little hint of the mind that was always active and planning the next move. Where others saw apparently unimportant and disconnected details, he had long since mastered the art of putting every clue in place and forming fast and accurate estimates of people and situations. He now signaled for a stop, and the party thankfully welcomed the opportunity to rest.

Ray looked at Dorothy, his wife, a gentle creature for these conditions, but who had an inner core of strength invisible to the casual observer. She rode her pony well and looked at home on it, but Ray did not miss the telltale lines of fatigue on her face.

"How are you, Dorothy?"

"Fine. Just a little tired, of course, but don't worry about me." It was the reply Ray expected. She would not buckle easily, but Ray dared not overestimate her powers of endurance.

Ray spoke a few words of encouragement to the four carriers and then he carefully examined each pony. He made sure that their loads were still well secured, but spent more time checking each animal. That done, he walked back to Dorothy and stretched himself on the ground beside her.

"Do you have any idea how much further it is, my dear?"

"Well, as you know, we were at 3,000 feet when we left Meng Ting an hour after sunrise. It is now about 3:00. First we passed the Shan villages, then the Kachins, and lastly the Wa. Each tribe lives at a certain altitude, give or take 500 feet. Judging from that, the time we have been traveling, and the condition of the carriers and the ponies, we must be at almost 10,000 feet. You will have noticed that there has been less and less talking among the carriers. The reason, of course, is that at this altitude they do not have enough breath left for talking. These men and animals are not as used to this altitude as we are. You can see that the trail is getting much steeper. I calculate it must be the last steep climb to the razor-sharp peak. The Lahu always live in high valleys, never on the peaks. If I'm right, I estimate it will take a half hour of very steep climbing and then another half hour downhill. About an hour altogether."

"Well, that's not too bad. How are the ponies?"

"One looks in very poor shape and might not make the next steep climb. If it collapses we will have to distribute his load onto the others, but I'm afraid they will not be able to take the extra weight. That's why I have been walking to keep my pony fairly fresh so that if the carrier pony does give out, mine can take its load." He made it sound optimistic. Actually, what Ray did not tell Dorothy was that more than one pony looked in bad shape; what would happen if several ponies collapsed? Their position would be desperate. He himself was good for hours, and with care, days if necessary. He could walk out and get help, but that would mean leaving Dorothy alone at the mercy of the jungle at night. That he would not do—though he knew she would not panic.

"Well, we must get moving, for when we rest too long our muscles can stiffen."

The party began to move and Ray set a relatively slow pace to conserve energy. Occasionally a monkey chattered, an exotic bird screeched, a startled snake wriggled away into the undergrowth. Apart from the creaking of the ropes that fastened the loads to the ponies, and occasional grunts from the carriers, silence reigned. During the day the jungle slept. It was at night that it came alive as animals crept to drinking holes and preyed on each other.

It was well that it wasn't the monsoon season, he reflected, or they would not have made it this far. Up they toiled, up what he hoped would be the last steep grind. After another half hour the trail began to fall away sharply. Gradually the jungle began to thin out and soon they were in sunshine.

"Ray, your estimate was exactly right," said Dorothy.

"It's nice to be correct sometimes," he replied with his slow smile.

Again he called a halt but only so that he could survey the scene ahead. In front of them was a valley surrounded by hillsides covered with highland rice fields and then a cluster of huts, perhaps thirty of them. There was no street; the ground was far too rough for that. The huts were simple structures made of mud and bamboo with thatched roofs. They stood on stilts to protect them from flash floods. In some places the jungle was only ten yards from the huts. Under and around most of the simple huts were a few pigs, goats, and chickens. The floors were made of bamboo lashed together but with inevitable cracks through which crumbs of food fell to be snatched up by chickens and grunting pigs. The tribal people did not like the dark, and the cracks in the floor served as a convenience when the call of nature had to be answered during the night. There was one hut just as simple as the others but slightly larger and much cleaner, and with no animals. Ray looked at it with a surge of relief. It was the home of Allyn and Leila Cooke, their friends. It was only 4:00 in the afternoon but the shadows of the towering mountains of the Yunnan Province of China were falling over parts of the little valley.

"Well, Dorothy, the Cookes are home," said Ray as he saw some smoke from a fire curling idly upward.

"We made it, and soon we will be with them and the ponies will get plenty of feed and rest . . . they deserve it; and I will not be sorry to get some myself."

Dorothy smiled her agreement and, in fact, the whole party seemed to take on a new lease of life. They followed the path that wound down and threaded through the jungle and village gardens.

Soon Allyn Cooke came striding toward them with his outstretched hand to give a warm greeting.

"Welcome, Ray and Dorothy. Some of your party look the worse for wear. You must tell us about your journey, but first come in and make yourselves at home. Leila will be happy to see you, and my Lahu helper will show your men where they can get feed for the animals."

Ray gave instructions to his carriers and he knew the animals and men would be well looked after.

"Before I come inside I would like to clean up a little." Ray walked over to where a tin basin stood on top of an old box and was glad to see that Allyn had already poured some water into it. By this time a few curious children had gathered around to look at the new arrivals. Ray rinsed his face, arms, hands, and neck. Refreshed, he climbed the crude steps into the house.

"I already feel like a new man," said Ray as he followed Allyn up the five rough wooden steps.

"Here, take this chair," said Allyn. "For once we have a special treat—some tea has just arrived from Shanghai. Would you like a cup?"

"No, thanks, I never drink the stuff," said Ray with a grin. "Make it water, please."

"And you, Dorothy?" he asked.

"Your water will taste good. We have had enough warm water from our canteens."

"I wish I could offer you ice," laughed Allyn, "but it's five years since I've seen any. Anyway, the water is fairly cool despite the fact it has been boiled."

Soon they were enjoying the large glasses of water and feeling relaxed.

"Where did you start from today?" asked Allyn.

"We spent the night in a Buddhist monastery in Meng Ting Valley. It's a stiff climb up here and my carriers and ponies are not used to this altitude."

Allyn frowned slightly. "We never stay in those valleys—too much malaria. Only this week one of our villagers spent the night at Meng Ting and today he has come down with what I think is cerebral malaria."

A change came over Ray in a flash. His relaxed attitude vanished and was replaced by alert concern. He was a skilled paramedic so he asked, "Can I see this man?"

"Of course. He's only about seventy-five yards away." Allyn led the way with Dorothy and Ray following. Ray carried a small black bag. All three picked their way expertly over the rough ground.

Allyn called out a greeting as he climbed the steps into the hut. The family was wailing with grief. Allyn spoke to them briefly and kindly and led the way to a part of the hut that was surrounded by a screen. Allyn parted the screen, and on the bed, which was little more than a collection of ragged clothes and mats, was the figure of a man, ominously still. Was he dead or alive?

Without a word Ray took in the situation at a glance, kneeled down, and instantly placed his fingers on the wrist of the man. His pulse was weak and irregular. His hot forehead confirmed the fact he had a raging fever.

"It's cerebral malaria all right," he said to Allyn, "and he is now in a coma. He'll be dead in perhaps two hours. As he is in a coma we cannot give him anything by mouth . . . but I have just the right thing." Even as he was speaking he took a syringe out of his black medicine bag and prepared to give the patient an injection in the buttock.

"But, Ray—you don't understand, you can't do that. The man has no money."

"What do you mean, I can't give him a shot?"

"He has no money," repeated Allyn.

"This is an emergency; he will soon be dead without this shot. You mean that money is more important than a human life?"

"I'm sorry, Ray, but our policy is to give no medicine unless the person can pay." Allyn looked miserable. "We have our policies. I did not make them but I have to obey them."

"Policies!" Ray could not keep the outrage and contempt out of his voice. "What good are policies? How can you talk about policies when life and death are involved?"

Allyn, tall, dark, intense, and with a stoop, had an artistic temperament. He was a very gifted musician and artist and had difficulty in remaining calm, but he stubbornly maintained his position. "Mr. Frazer made our rules and he is my superintendent; I do as I am told. Do you think I enjoy this?"

For a few moments they froze in position.

Rapidly and calmly Ray weighed his options, much as he had often done in his days in competitive running. He was a man of action but never allowed his emotion to affect his judgment. How long would it take to give the injection? The preparations had been made; twenty seconds and it would be over. Then he looked around and with a sinking heart realized that they had an audience. Neighbors and family had gathered. Ray and Allyn had talked in English, but the observant Lahu would have noticed the rising tension and concluded that this was a confrontation—and that was bad.

Ray was shattered. With a feeling of desperation he realized that there was only one way out. He had often known disappointments and great obstacles in the past. Now he was the guest of another missionary and of another mission, the China Inland Mission. Never before had he accepted defeat tamely, but now there was no other way.

He reached out his hand and Allyn grasped it with both of his. It was a gesture of warmth and understanding.

"I'm sorry, Allyn, I don't know what came over me. The

thought of a man dying when I could save him was just too much."

"I know how you feel; it's been a bad day for me too, watching him sinking, and I am not a skilled paramedic like you are."

"I hope I haven't damaged your work."

"Don't worry, your handshake and apology took care of that and I will explain it to our brothers and neighbors."

He turned to the small group and spoke clearly in their Lahu language. "The day is late and my dear friends Mr. and Mrs. Buker have been traveling for many days all the way from Lashio. They should be resting, but Mr. Buker heard that our friend was so ill, and he wanted to help." Seeing that he could turn the confrontation into a lesson, he continued, "In my country beyond the great ocean Mr. Buker is a famous man and an honored teacher as well as a man skillful with medicine. Now you have seen that he is a great Jesus man. Now Mr. and Mrs. Buker must come to our home and eat and rest, but when we get there the first thing we will do is pray for our friend Mong Ting-Chang. Our great God can heal and He has promised to hear our prayers, so I urge you who are Jesus' followers to pray also."

Ray slowly packed his syringe back into his bag, and even though he understood how expertly Allyn had handled the situation he felt emotionally drained and dejected. They walked out slowly; Ray did not dare look back at the patient.

They made their way to the Lahu hut that was the Cookes' home and as they walked Ray could feel Allyn's arm around his shoulders. It was a gesture that would not be missed by a single witness.

After a time of prayer for the sick victim Mong Ting-Chang, the Cookes showed the Bukers into the simple bedroom that was reserved for guests.

When the Bukers were alone, Ray turned to Dorothy and said, "I don't understand myself. Only once before have I ever felt so indignant. . . ."

"Yes, and that was when we were at Bates College, and the Dean would not allow Benny Mays to debate against Oxford University simply because he was black." The gentle, understanding Dorothy finished the sentence for him.

"Then I was a boy; now I am a man. I should have avoided a public spectacle like that," responded Ray.

"Raymond, my dear, you are being too hard on yourself. I have told you for months that you have been overworked and have pleaded with you to take a rest. Besides that, even I was shocked that you were not allowed to save the life of Ting-Chang."

"I still cannot understand the strange rules of the China Inland Mission."

"Neither can I, but remember that we came to learn why their methods are so much more effective than ours in the American Baptist Mission." Then with a typical woman's touch of common sense and with the knowledge that she had talked more than was usual for her, she added, "Come now, dear, we must not be late for dinner."

After they had eaten their meal, Ray asked Allyn if he would play the violin for them. He readily agreed to do so and walked over to the violin case that looked battered from much use. There was nothing battered about the violin, which he lovingly lifted from its case. Even in the relatively poor light, the warm luster of the polished wood spoke of great care. After Allyn had tuned it, he asked the Bukers what they would like him to play.

"I don't know what you can play; I have only heard that you have a great musical gift," replied Ray.

"I'm not so sure about a great musical gift," laughed Allyn. "Do you like classical music?"

"Oh, yes!" Ray and Dorothy chorused.

Soon they were entranced as they listened to the "First Brandenburg Concerto" by Bach.

"Now Leila must play," said Allyn.

She walked over to the little portable organ and said, "I

wish I could have brought my piano to China as Allyn brought his violin."

Soon they were listening to the haunting music of Beethoven's "Moonlight Sonata." The Bukers marveled at how gifted the Cookes were and expressed their appreciation. Outwardly Ray seemed calm and attentive, but inwardly he was emotionally torn apart as he thought about Ting-Chang. Only Dorothy could sense the turmoil raging within him.

"If you think we have musical gifts, wait until you hear Mr. Frazer. What he can get out of a portable organ still amazes us," Allyn said. "But now it's time for you to get some rest. Tomorrow I will tell you how we use our music in the work among the Lahu. It's not only a pleasure, but Mr. Frazer has turned it into a marvelous tool in teaching them spiritual truth."

Soon Ray and Dorothy were in their bedroom. Ray sat on the bed, dazed from all the activities of the day. Presently he broke the silence, "I have never met a couple whom I feel so close to . . . outside of my brother Dick and his wife."

"I know how you feel," responded Dorothy. "What spiritual giants they are. I can sense the peace in this home."

"I wish I could understand their rules. I can't forget Ting-Chang. By morning he will be dead; in fact, he may be dead already. Cerebral malaria can kill in two hours—and to think I could have saved his life."

"Well, dear, you did all you could; the rest we must leave with God."

They went to bed, but sleep would not come quickly to Ray. Being a skillful paramedic had its burdens as well as its blessings; and defeat had a bitter taste.

Ray was always an early riser, but the next morning he rose earlier than usual only to discover that Allyn had already washed and shaved. Outwardly Ray appeared calm and serene but he had been deeply affected by the events of the day before, as he was always hurt by any afflictions of his beloved Lahu.

"How is Ting-Chang?" As Ray asked the question, he dreaded the reply.

"I have just come from him. He is much better, and is walking about."

"What did you do, Allyn?"

"Well, we all prayed, didn't we?"

Ray felt like a little schoolboy, but a great wave of relief and wonder swept over him. "I must tell Dorothy."

It was a grateful group that gave thanks before they ate their simple breakfast.

Ray had received thousands of picture post cards from supporters in the USA, and had discovered that simple tribespeople took a childlike delight in receiving them. Therefore he often used them to help him make friends.

He gave them away to the Lahu, and because of his knowledge of the Lahu language he soon had a growing group of children and adults surrounding him. The combined use of the pictures and humor, he discovered, soon broke down barriers with strangers. It was one of the aspects of missionary work in which he excelled and also enjoyed.

After a short time Allyn Cooke walked up to him and spoke in a low voice, "Ray, I hate to say this, but we would prefer you did not give these post cards away."

Ray had heard missionaries of his own mission ridicule the policies of the China Inland Mission in the Yunnan Province, and there flashed through his mind the thought that perhaps their criticism was justified, but he pushed the idea aside. After all, even though this visit to the Cookes had been to enjoy Christian fellowship, Dorothy had reminded him that it was also to learn why the work among the Lisu and the Lahu had been so successful.

He heard himself saying, "But why, they cost me nothing

and I have thousands more of them back home in Meng Meng."

"I certainly see how skillfully you use them," replied Allyn, "and I envy you your gift of making friends so quickly, but it's simply a matter of principle. We give absolutely nothing free to our Lahu, except our teaching and ourselves. We do not want them to become grasping and greedy. We want them to stand on their own feet and to depend on the Lord."

Seeing the bewilderment on Ray's face, Allyn said, "Ray, it's time we had a talk and I explained to you our policies and how we came to develop them. I really should not say 'we,' because it was our field superintendent, Mr. James O. Frazer, who adopted them. When I first came out from the States, the work among the Lisu was relatively well established, and I simply continued his work in the way he had pioneered it and applied it to the Lahu when I was put in charge. God has marvelously blessed this man's work, Ray." They slowly walked back to the hut and sat on the small porch. Allyn began telling Ray the story of the remarkable missionary—James O. Frazer.

It was a great help that the Cookes were fellow Americans, and the Bukers and they were on a first-name basis. They could come to the point more quickly than with their English friends. They were also approximately the same age. There the similarities ended because the Cookes had not gone to a college, although they had attended the Bible Institute of Los Angeles (Biola). Ray was eager to learn, so Allyn found that Ray listened with rapt attention as he talked of his love of James Frazer and the work that Frazer pioneered.

Frazer was enormously gifted in the field of music and that was one of the many things he gladly sacrificed in his love for the Lord and His service. He was eventually to die at the relatively early age of 53, in the year 1938.

He applied to and was accepted by the China Inland Mission at the age of twenty-one, without formal theological training, but with an honors degree in engineering from London University. The mission eventually sent him to the mountainous area of China where he quickly developed a love for the Lisu, men of the high country, who had been unreached with the gospel. The combination of a musical ear and a flair for math were an enormous help in his linguistic work. He was certainly no revolutionary but he learned from his mistakes. One important example illustrates this. He became heartbroken when he learned that his first few converts among the Lisu so often returned to their old heathen ways. His solution was a radical one for a Westerner. He saw that it was almost impossible for one Christian to thrive spiritually when subjected to every form of abuse and harassment from his family and village. Frazer then made a policy that he would not baptize a Christian who stood alone in his faith, but would work and pray until a whole family and later whole villages were ready to burn their "spirit shelves" at which they worshiped and apply for baptism. This was a dramatic break from the typical evangelical emphasis on the conversion of the individual, and many colleagues thought he was wrong. His method was vindicated when later scores of entire villages turned to Christ, and Lisu by the thousands became Christians.

As Allyn talked the time flew, and it was time for the evening meal. Allyn continued to tell one story after another to illustrate the various policies they adopted. Ray learned, for example, that if pastors or evangelists were needed, their own people were expected to support them and they received nothing from mission funds. Even when Frazer traveled and needed carriers, the Lisu Christians regarded it a privilege to help the man they loved dearly, and who had brought the gospel to them.

They discussed music, and Allyn explained that Mr. Frazer had written many hymns and that these had been a useful way of teaching the Lisu and Lahu much spiritual truth. Ray told them that he had no gift for music such as

Allyn and Leila had, but that Dorothy often used a concertina to teach hymns among the Lahu tribe with whom they worked. He went on to explain that their Lahu loved music and were very good with it.

"So are the Lisu," said Allyn. "Do you know that Mr. Frazer has taught them to sing Handel's *Messiah?*"

"That must be wonderful," exclaimed Ray. "I wish I could do that with our Lahu."

"I'll come and teach the Lahu to sing it."

"That really would be great if you could spare the time, Allyn," said Dorothy.

"I'll make time."

Taking a book from one of his shelves, Allyn asked Ray if he had ever seen a copy. It was titled *Missionary Methods: St. Paul's or Ours?* written by Roland Allen.

Ray took the book and quickly read the Table of Contents, and then turned to Chapter Six which dealt with finances. As he rapidly skimmed the pages, he said, "This is great, but I've never heard of it before."

"Neither had I until I bought it on our last furlough."

Ray made a careful note of the title, author, and publisher. "I will order a copy when I get back to Meng Meng. Of course, it will take months to reach me, but it's just the sort of book I need. In fact, I'll order two because my twin brother, Dick, will want one also.

"I can now see the reasons for your policies, but surely there is room for flexibility such as with Ting-Chang."

"He is healed now, isn't he?"

"Oh, come, Allyn, you know that does not change the need to show compassion."

"Well, if you make exceptions, where do you stop? Other exceptions will then be made and the basic principle will be shattered."

"I still think that the policies are good, but as I think of our own work I believe that I would build more flexibility into them."

Allyn laughed. "I have been so busy talking about our own work that I have completely ignored yours. How is it going at Meng Meng?"

"We see some encouraging things, but because of the Great Depression back home I no longer have money to pay the pastors, and whole villages are going back to heathenism. It's heartbreaking."

"But don't you see that would not happen in our work because, beginning with the Lisu, and now with the Lahu, we never gave them money in the first place."

"Yes, I see that, but remember we have a great deal of medical work in Burma. What would the British government think if we stood by and let a man die when we could have saved his life?"

"I know that would be a colossal problem, but we did not establish hospitals to begin with."

"Just remember that our hospitals were in existence nearly one hundred years ago. Your work is comparatively new."

"Obviously, I cannot say what Mr. Frazer would have done, but you do see where your policies are leading you."

"Yes, I don't pretend that our policies have worked out well, but you can imagine the uproar that would take place if I suddenly changed the methods that we have developed since 1813 and completely changed to your program. I have to find a way to modify our procedures but still preserve some flexibility."

"I see you have immense problems. In a sense you are locked into a system that you may not be able to change, but prayer is going to be important as well as careful thinking and planning," Allyn concluded.

After three days the Bukers had to continue their journey. Their men and animals were rested and well fed. The visit had been all too brief, but both of the missionary families appreciated the warm friendship that developed. As they parted Allyn prayed that the Bukers would have a safe journey across the mountains where bandits posed a continuous threat.

Soon they were out of the village and climbing the mountains as steep as the roofs of many New England homes. A detour had been made to visit the Cookes and now the Bukers had to continue their journey to Meng Meng, two mountain ranges away. Ray was in the lead as usual, with Dorothy behind, followed by the pack animals.

For much of the way home Ray was very deep in thought. Dorothy, in her understanding way, left him to think on all the experiences he had been through with the Cookes and the lessons he had learned. He certainly had much food for thought.

From time to time his mind flashed back to the three famous seminaries in which he had studied. No man could have taken more trouble and effort to prepare himself for a missionary career. He thought of his eight long years in the study of Greek, and that was no mistake, for it was such a great help in his translation work. It seemed strange that J. O. Frazer with no formal theological training had been so much more successful than Ray had been with the Lahu. This did not make him jealous; quite the contrary, he respected Frazer all the more.

What about the nine years of track, culminating with his Olympic gold medal? That had been marvelous preparation for the rigors of pioneer work in the mountains of Burma and Yunnan. His wonderful home in the New England parsonage had also been perfect training.

He could clearly see the advantages of the methods that J. O. Frazer had developed, but he could not see how he could incorporate them into the rigid patterns of work that had been inherited in the American Baptist Mission.

No, God had guided him thus far and He would continue to do so. Ray had to continue the learning process, and to leave no stone unturned in his search to improve his own work. The Cookes had shown him some principles, and he resolved to learn much more from them, and perhaps even from Frazer himself. How wonderful it would be if he could meet the man who had been so successful in the tribal work of Yunnan.

The years ahead would bring new problems, but this visit had been immensely satisfying. Ray journeyed on with new hope and courage.

# 1

# BEGINNINGS

On Sunday morning August 27, 1899, at 4:00 A.M. identical twins were born to the wife of a Baptist pastor in Foster, Rhode Island. The news did not take long to reach the whole community, for it consisted of only three homes, including the parsonage. When Mrs. Buker realized that she had given birth to twins, her comment was, "I might as well die."

History has not recorded what the pastor preached on that day, or what his reaction was at having two more children to feed on a very limited budget. Richard Steele Buker was born fifteen minutes before Raymond Bates. There was not the slightest visible difference in appearance between them, so to differentiate them, one wore a pink ribbon and the other a blue one. It was claimed that one day the ribbons were accidently removed, resulting in a mixup of the twins' identification. Their mother laughed at such an idea. There was evidently no doubt in her mind! This similarity was to cause confusion all their lives, and even when they were well into their seventies they cheerfully exploited it for humor. A missionary who knows Ray Buker well had spent some time with him in Denver in 1977. Shortly afterward when in Wheaton, seeing Ray's familiar form, he said, "Well, Dr. Buker, I certainly appreciated the time we had together in Denver." Dr. Buker replied cheerfully, "We were certainly glad to have you!" Only later was the missionary advised that Ray Buker was still in Denver, and that the man he had greeted so warmly was, in fact, his brother Richard (Dick).

The home into which Dick and Ray were born seems to have been a remarkably happy one. This owed nothing to material possessions but rather to the remarkable character of the parents and children. Their father had the oversight of three small churches. He was also superintendent of the town schools, and for all this he was paid less than $600 a year. Even though the dollar was worth much more then, this amount was not adequate to feed and clothe a large family. The twins joined a family of two sisters and three brothers, and another sister was born later. To help feed the family of ten, their father farmed the land belonging to the parsonage.

The Buker family were of old New England stock. In 1680 several Buker families had come from Sweden and settled in Scituate, Massachusetts. In 1701 the Bukers moved to York, Maine. A James Buker was born on February 22, 1768, and is listed on the Bowdoin tax list. He married a Ruth Rogers who was born on March 22, 1770, and who had come from a pioneer family of Georgetown, Maine. The great-grandfather of the twins was Caleb Buker. Though a successful farmer and a captain in the Militia, he died at the young age of forty, after his wife Lydia had given him seven children.

The sixth child was a boy named Samuel Cotton Buker, born on June 2, 1826. He was to become the father of four children, including Fred Marshall Buker, the father of the twins. In later years, in tough athletic competition and in pioneering in Burma, the very qualities of endurance and courage that were so much a part of this New England family were to be put to the extreme test in the lives of Raymond and Richard.

The father of the twins, Fred, did not plan to be a pastor but rather a teacher. He was educated at Bates College in Lewiston, Maine, and during his last winter term at Bates he attended a lecture given under the auspices of the Young Men's Christian Association, of which he was the president. A faculty member of Cobb Divinity School, Professor Howe, had a talk with him about going on to divinity school. Fred Buker replied that he did not feel called to preach. "What do you consider a call?" asked Mr. Howe. Fred told him that he was not sure and asked the professor to explain his views. Professor Howe pointed out that a candidate for the ministry should have a fairly good education and a capacity for holding people's attention. He urged Fred to consider the ministry.

Later, Fred Buker had a conversation with Dr. Fullerton, the president of Cobb Divinity School, and was able to tell the professor that he had put himself into God's hand for his future service. Dr. Fullerton assured him that if God wanted him to enter the Christian ministry, He would make it known. That coincided exactly with the convictions of Fred Buker, and future events confirmed this.

His first teaching post as assistant principal at Green Mountain Seminary in Waterbury, Vermont, provided a yearly salary of $400 plus room and board. After a year it was increased to $500. When we compare this with his salary later as a pastor, with eight children to provide for, we see the financial sacrifice he made when he eventually entered the ministry.

As a teacher he was prepared to accept invitations to preach as and when the opportunity presented itself. He did not have long to wait. Following a three-weeks' teaching period, Fred was asked to fill the pulpit of Rev. Ezra Fuller while the pastor attended the Vermont Free Will Baptist yearly meeting. When faced with the request that he announce to the congregation that he would be preaching again the following Sunday, Fred's reticence prompted him to say he would "take charge," reflecting his feeling that "preaching" was too grand a description for his abilities.

Like thousands of preachers before and since, he agonized over his preparation. He tried to prepare a sermon on, "Verily, verily, I say unto thee, Except a man be born anew, he cannot see the kingdom of God." After much labor he despaired of his efforts and searched for a sermon preached by someone else that he could read. Nothing seemed suitable, so he preached from the text he had originally chosen. Several members of the church let it be known that they wished he would preach every Sunday, so he was off to a good start on his preaching vocation.

He was later asked to fill the pulpit for four Sundays while the pastor was on vacation, and he soon reached the limit of his resources for preaching. So it's no wonder he was delighted to see the pastor return. Alas, the following Friday evening he received an urgent note from the pastor. He had to leave town to take a funeral service and he asked Fred to preach one more Sunday. He had obviously received good reports. So, on Saturday Fred Buker labored once again in preparation, and preached for the fifth successive Sunday.

Some months later he was invited to preach the baccalaureate sermon. Quite a beginning for a man who felt no call to the ministry.

That year the Bukers went to Lewiston, Maine, for their vacation. Fred again met Professor Howe and the professor asked Fred if he intended to continue teaching; Fred replied that he did. The professor took a telegram from his pocket that requested a preacher for the following Sunday at Rochester, New Hampshire. Fred asked, "Isn't there someone in the divinity school who would be more qualified than I?" The professor replied that he did not know of a single man he would rather send—a significant compliment. Professor Howe commented that he had preached there the previous Sunday, and because he was acknowledged to be one of the finest preachers in the divinity school, this gave Fred much food for thought. He promised to give Professor Howe his decision the following morning.

It would have been easy to decline, but the conviction grew that if he went, he might help someone. He accepted the invitation and traveled to Rochester by train on Saturday afternoon. He was met at the station by two members of the church committee and escorted to the home of a Mr. Preston.

The morning service went very well and Fred felt much at ease and enjoyed preaching. While eating lunch, Mr. Preston asked him about his plans for preaching in the future, but Fred replied that he intended to continue his teaching career. Mr. Preston then told him that the church had called a man to be their new pastor, but they did not know if he would accept the invitation. He added that if the man refused the invitation, the church committee was anxious that Fred Buker become the new pastor. The man they had called did accept the invitation, however, and that closed that door. But invitations to preach in various churches continued to come to Fred, and the favorable reactions seemed to confirm Professor Howe's opinion and to point toward Fred's future career.

Sabattus, Maine, was his parent's home during this time and while visiting them one week in 1890 Fred discovered that their church was without a pastor. The committee asked him to preach for one Sunday, and after hearing him, invited him to preach for the next six Sundays.

In the fall Fred Buker returned to Waterbury for the new school year. That year the Vermont Free Will Baptist yearly meeting was to be held in Waterbury. In an unusual action he was invited to preach at the meeting and also at the local Methodist church on Sunday morning. The recognition of his preaching gift was obvious, but his own diffidence remained.

During the academic year 1890–91, the pastor of the Free Baptist Church at Waterbury left his pastorate to accept a call from another church. Fred Buker was asked to take his place for the remainder of the school year in addition to his teaching duties. This appointment involved a good deal of responsibility for a young man of twenty-four without any theological training.

To regularize things, he withdrew his membership from Sabattus to the church in Waterbury. He absented himself from the church meeting at which his membership was considered, and during the following week he was asked if he knew what action had been taken, and his reply was no. He was then told that his membership had been accepted and the clerk had been instructed to ask the Huntington quarterly meeting to give Fred Buker a license to preach. Astounded, he asked who had given them the authority to do that, only to receive the reply, "We got our authority from on High." Three weeks later he attended the Huntington quarterly meeting. The committee on licenses examined him and voted to license him. He continued teaching but also preached in the Waterbury church every Sunday.

At the end of the academic year, changes were made in the administration of his school and he was asked to become the principal. This invitation to one so young was a real compliment, but he declined and left the school. It seems likely that he had begun to appreciate his preaching gift and was concerned that increased administrative responsibility would interfere with his preaching.

In June his license to preach automatically expired, but he deliberately absented himself from the quarterly meeting in case it might appear that he wanted the license renewed. His new license arrived two weeks later in the mail. He now found himself at a crossroads in his life. He had given up his position at Green Mountain Seminary and faced the future jobless. He sought various opportunities in the teaching profession, but nothing opened. He began to ask himself whether it was not possible that God was calling him into fulltime ministry. It was not widely known that he was a licensed preacher. He wrote to a church at South Stafford, Vermont, that needed a pastor, but they had called a new pastor just before his letter arrived.

Having received information from a friend that two small churches in Wheelock, Vermont, needed a pastor, Fred inquired about them. A prompt invitation to preach for a week gave him opportunity to minister at both the Wheelock Village Church and the South Wheelock Church. It was with a great sense of challenge that Fred accepted the call a short time later to pastor both churches.

In the Baptist church at Waterbury was a young lady named Ellen Fedelia Wilder. She had been a student at Green Mountain Seminary and Fred Buker had been one of her teachers. She had heard him preach his first sermon and was one of many who was impressed, and was known to have commented that she could listen to him preach every Sunday.

In temperament she was quite unlike Fred. She was vigorous, outgoing, had a keen sense of humor, and was known as a tomboy. While she was a student at Green Mountain, she was late in returning to school and missed his assignment in algebra. As a result, he gave her a particularly hard test which she passed with flying colors.

During Ellen's second year at seminary, she invited the faculty to her home for a party at which she proved to be a good hostess. During this party Fred Buker said to himself, "I am going to marry her one day." They had, of course, seen a good deal of each other at school and in the church.

Much of the summer of 1891 he spent at her home in Waitsfield, Vermont, helping with the harvesting, and on August 19 they were married. They planned a honeymoon trip to his home at Sabattus, Maine, but Fred was greatly troubled by an ulcerated tooth and the trip had to be cancelled.

That fall he began his ministry at Wheelock, Vermont, and a year later, in August 1892, their first child was born, a boy whom they named Harold.

In 1893 Fred was ordained and later that year they moved to Sandwich, New Hampshire, where he was to become the pastor of the church there. It was here in 1894 that Sibyl, their second child, was born, and another daughter, Mary, was born in 1895. Waterbury, Vermont, was their next home and here two more sons were born, Kenneth in 1896 and Gerald in 1897.

The family left Vermont in May of 1898 to begin a pastorate in Foster, Rhode Island. Fred was pastor of the "Line Church," so named because it was on the dividing line between Rhode Island and Connecticut. The Line could hardly be called a village as it consisted of the parsonage and church on one side of the road, which was in Rhode Island, and a store on the other side of the road, which was in Connecticut. When the telephone came to that area, there was no connection over the state line. So if someone in Rhode Island wanted to give a message to a person in Connecticut, he would phone a message to the parsonage and then someone would have to cross the road to the other telephone and send the message.

It was here that the twins were born on Sunday, August 27, 1899, and where they spent their first ten years.

## Elementary School Days

The world was rapidly changing at the turn of the century when the twins were born. In Europe the great powers were seizing colonial territories with great abandon and the USA, which had always felt superior to these countries who had great territorial ambitions, discovered that the fever was infectious. A wave spread across the nation demanding that it join the scramble for colonial power, a wave that was opposed in vain by many who felt that it was a denial of the very principles on which the republic was founded.

The country had been greatly influenced by the writings of the great naval historian Mahan, and events crowded on each other. On February 15, 1898, the armored cruiser USS *Maine* blew up in Havanna Harbor, Cuba, with the loss of 260 lives. In April of that year the US declared war on Spain.

Five days later Admiral Dewey steamed into Manila Bay and issued the famous command, "You may fire when ready, Gridley." Thus began armed action in the Philippines.

The year the twins were born, Joseph Stilwell (Vinegar Joe of later fame) was still in high school in Yonkers, New York. The names of both the twins and Stilwell were to be indelibly linked with Burma some forty years later. None of these events made any impact on the full and bustling parsonage in Rhode Island. When Fred Buker first went to Foster, Rhode Island, he had charge of only one church, the "Line Church." Later he also took over the "Morning Star Church" in the north of the town for two years. After those years he gave up the pastorate of the Morning Star Church but accepted the pastorate of Moosup Valley Church and also of Rice City Church. As he was still the pastor of the Line Church, he was now responsible for three churches. In addition, he became superintendent of the Foster schools. As we mentioned earlier, for all this he received the princely sum of $600 annually, plus the use of the parsonage. It is obvious that the father was an exceedingly busy man and a relatively poor one. Fortunately, his wife had a resilient spirit and kept her brood well looked after and disciplined. One year, however, she became somewhat depressed when Thanksgiving drew near and she had no chickens for the Thanksgiving dinner. Two different people brought chickens, four in all, and others brought apples, produce, and a fruitcake. This food not only helped to meet their needs, but it also revealed the affection with which they were regarded by the members of their congregation. This affection was to be characteristic of the life and ministry of Fred Buker wherever he served.

The parsonage consisted of two stories plus an attic. The one-hundred-and-twenty-year-old church consisted of only one room. The Sunday school classes were held in various corners of the building, and outside if the weather was suitable. There were sheds behind the church in which horse teams were kept during the service. As is still the case in many New England Baptist churches, there was no baptistry, but new converts waited for the summer and were baptized in a local stream or pond. "Close to nature," comments Ray, and indeed they were close to nature all their early lives.

Foster could not actually be called a village, so people came from the farms and houses in the surrounding countryside to attend the church. The horse sheds were favorite places for play and Ray recalls with a chuckle that it was there he received his first kiss. On being asked whether or not he took the initiative, he shook his head vigorously. "No, it was the girl. She was a year older than I."

Ray began to develop a lasting love for the countryside, although he was not yet knowledgeable as to the names of plants, trees, and flowers. That kind of knowledge he developed much later in life. He feels that one of the great advantages of a rural childhood was that it automatically gave him an insight into the psychology of country people that was invaluable to him in his future ministry.

The twins' early years were full of outdoor activities. They kept busy helping their father with his limited amount of farming. The first paying job they had was carrying wood for a widow who lived nearby, at the rate of fifteen cents a week. From this sum a tithe was always allocated for the Lord's work. When asked if they had any hobbies, Ray commented, "We were too busy. We needed money."

From the age of eleven, he avidly sought ways to earn money—trapping rabbits at fifteen cents apiece; taking cows back and forth to pasture for one dollar per month; mowing lawns at ten cents per hour; shoveling snow, sawdust, or shavings; and paper routes. Ray confesses that sometimes much of the paper route profits were spent at the corner drugstore. Ice cream cones cost five cents, sundaes ten cents, and banana splits fifteen cents. Three or four of the brothers had paper routes and their mother was the treasurer. Ray feels that it must have been very frustrating for his mother to know that some of the profits were used before they were surrendered to her. It was during this period that Ray developed an overpowering appetite for ice cream, which still persists! Apart from splurging on ice cream, their earnings were used to buy items such as clothes or a bicycle, while their parents provided room and board. Even later when they worked in the Kittery, New Hampshire, Navy Yard, 1918–19, the twins lived at home so that they could save their money for college expenses, commuting the ten miles to work.

A one-room country schoolhouse was the location of the twins' early education at age seven. As a disciplinarian in the home, Mrs. Buker, supported by her husband, provided a routine that included completion of school assignments before outdoor playtime, and departure for bed at an early hour, which was rarely appreciated by the children. At eight years of age, Ray began to record his daily activities in a diary. From his bedroom window one evening, he saw his parents walking down the road to visit neighbors. In a childish hand he inscribed: "Our parents don't love us; they leave us. It is terrible!"

In the energy of their young years, the twins raced each other home from school. Dick commented that this began the development of body, enabling them both to succeed in five- and six-mile cross-country contests in their college days. They were always to remember with gratitude a mother who loved and disciplined them, who made possible the significant achievement on the race track in the years that followed.

Certainly by today's standards the children had an upbringing that was rigid and very strict. Play was permitted after school assignments were finished, but there was always the necessity of work because the family income was so low.

As the twins grew older, certain places were "off limits." One was the church horse shed where, as Ray put it, "A good deal more than kissing took place between the fellows and girls!" From their earliest days, Sunday was rigidly observed.

The Buker children were dressed in their best clothes all day. They were required to attend Sunday school and all services. Certain books were specifically set aside for Sunday reading and the family took walks together. At the church services the children always occupied the rows near the front, right under the gaze of their father. Today many would believe that such a childhood would inevitably bring violent rebellion in later life. Significantly, quite the reverse took place. The children looked forward to Sundays and enjoyed their father's preaching. In later life Ray continued to observe the Lord's Day with a strong Puritan emphasis.

As an example, Ray spent at least one month for many years at summer camps. Others would go swimming on Sunday but Ray would not even consider doing so. Although he held this strong conviction himself, he never gave the slightest indication that he thought these convictions applied to others. He joked about it, but he never thought less of an individual because he held different views.

Ray's life and character will never be understood if we do not grasp the fact that he drew a strong distinction between things he considered to be basic and those that were peripheral. In later life he was often at the center of controversy. Because he was so tolerant and friendly others failed to understand that in him could be found a core of steel; and that there were central and crucial truths that he would always guard with kindness and tenacity. These truths he would defend no matter what personal sacrifice it involved.

A pleasure the children enjoyed on Sunday took place in the evening when their father was due home from preaching at one of the outer churches. On seeing him they would run to meet him, and after a joyful reunion they would be permitted to ride to the stable. Once a year each of the children was allowed to go with his father to one of the distant churches. Usually the pastor took only one child with him, but the twins were almost inseparable. They were also very small, so that when their turn came he was able to take both the twins in the horse-drawn buggy he now owned.

In 1910, when the twins were ten years old, their father accepted the call to a church in Contoocook, New Hampshire, so the family had to say good-by to their many friends and move. Contoocook is an Indian name, and there was an attractive stream running through the village. They were still living in a rural setting, but now they were in a village with a railroad station, several stores, and a high school. There was more opportunity now for the twins to earn money, and here there always seemed to be odd jobs for energetic children. Leading cows to pasture brought one dollar a month.

When Ray was twelve, he was at an evening prayer meeting where his father gave an invitation to follow Christ. Ray answered it, and his conversion dates from this time. It was no hurried decision; he had contemplated it for many weeks and had actually decided to publicize his faith before the meeting started. It did signify a real acceptance of Jesus Christ as Savior, but it was relatively superficial. A deep and complete consecration came later. Ray and Dick were baptized together in a local pond by their father.

During the next four years there were lapses and times when Ray felt ashamed of being the son of a minister. All too often in other families this has led to a rejection of a father's faith, but this extreme reaction did not take place in the lives of the twins.

Ray describes it as unique that their upbringing was puritanical, yet their parents exercised great skill in making home a happy place, and so avoided the kind of reaction that would probably have occurred if the control were harsh instead of loving and happy. Although their father was very busy, their parents insisted on taking much time for family devotions.

At the age of thirteen the twins took on a newspaper route delivering the *Manchester Union.* At fourteen they spent much of their summer mowing lawns on the huge estate of a local millionaire. This was very heavy and hard work for boys who were so small in stature. That September they had to spend a few days in bed before starting school, because the old, heavy lawnmower had proven to be very difficult for them. Ray has always believed that it was this exercise that helped to develop his barrellike chest which became a real asset in his astonishing athletic successes later on.

Because the twins were so small, they were not able to participate in the major school sports. This lack of height was not a family characteristic for their brothers were all taller, but at their maximum height the twins never surpassed 5'7''. Later this was to have totally unforeseen results.

Their father had become an excellent pastor. He was never to be in demand as a great conference speaker but he was skilled enough to hold the attention of all the children in the front row. To the twins his sermons were never boring or burdensome. He was marvelous at telling Bible stories, and used many illustrations and applications. He was not a great expositor as we would define that word today, but he had a ministry custom-made for his rural congregation. This preaching gift was accompanied by a genuine friendliness and by a saintly character. His popularity was such that when the twins were fifteen or sixteen, Ray can remember being troubled by the text, "Woe be unto you when all men speak well of you," as he recognized his father's popularity. This affection was found not merely among his church members but also in the community at large, although it did not prevent him from speaking out boldly and fearlessly on moral issues of the day.

## High School Days

The village of Contoocook had a small high school, so there were limitations as to what it could offer its students. The enrollment for the high school was fifty, and the class in which the twins enrolled in 1912 numbered fifteen.

Academically the twins had always done well, and much of this was due to the respect for learning that characterized their home. This included their mother's insistence on the priority of homework.

After two and two-thirds years in Contoocook High School, the twins transferred to Mount Hermon Boys' School in the third quarter of 1915. This was a large preparatory school for boys that had been opened by Dwight L. Moody in 1881. It was only a few miles across the border in Massachusetts. At this time World War I was raging in Europe and the United States would soon be drawn into it. For the twins who had always been accustomed to small villages, small schools and churches, the change was significant. Mount Hermon had massive buildings and a student body of six hundred. Here was a much greater challenge and a wider variety of courses from which they could select. It was here that Ray began a study of Greek that was to last eight years. This proved a great asset to him later in his translation work in Burma.

The twins were physically the smallest in their class and, as far as athletics were concerned, they were in the same position as before—too small for any team activities. However, there was one important difference; at Mount Hermon there was considerable emphasis on track and cross-country. Ray entered the two-mile race in the spring after two weeks of training. It was his first participation in a race, but he did well enough to take third place, and that gave his team one more point. His team, the Crossley Blues, won the meet by one point. The two-mile race was the last event of the day, and Ray was quite a hero! Running was a natural for the twins because all through their childhood, brimful of energy, they had run everywhere. Now, here at least was a sport that was organized and in which they could take part. They flung themselves into it with great zest. Ray could not sprint but he did have the dogged perseverance that enabled him to prevail in the longer distances. An early riser all his life, he had no trouble running two miles at 5:30 each morning.

In the fall of 1916, when Ray had just passed his seventeenth birthday, the term began with an ambitious program of cross-country races, five in all. His experience in the two-mile race in the spring encouraged Ray to enter all five cross-country races; the two-mile, two-and-a-half mile, four-and five-, and the last and most important, the six-mile, which was really too long for boys of his age. The six-mile race was a big occasion at Mount Hermon. One-third of the student body entered, numbering 200 boys, and medals were presented to the first three places. Dick Watson, the man in charge of the dining hall, was very enthusiastic about track and had twenty-five pies baked for the first twenty-five boys that finished. Ray won a place in the earlier events, so he had high hopes of being placed in the six-mile event. Before the race started, Ray studied the medals and decided that the second-place medal was the prettiest. This he hoped to get. At the end of the race, the second-place medal of silver inlay and blue lettering became his prized possession. The winner was Cecil Leath; he and Ray Buker were to race against each other many times in their college years, but Leath was never able to beat Ray again. He was an excellent runner, but he lacked the dogged self-discipline that made Ray train so well, and which eventually helped him to become an Olympic star.

At Mount Hermon everyone was required to be involved in a daily work period. Ray worked for two hours each afternoon on the school farm. His brother Dick, because he was experienced in milking, was given the job of a tester which involved milking the cows three or four times daily. The significant fact was that he had to get up at 4:00 in the morning so he could start the first milking at 4:30. He was as good a runner as Ray, but this exceptionally early rising took the edge off his running capabilities. He still trained and competed but could not match the performance of his twin. In the six-mile race in which Ray came in second,

Dick came in twenty-fifth, qualifying him for the last pie!

The twins spent a year at Mount Hermon from the third quarter of their junior year to the third quarter of their senior year. They then returned to Contoocook to join their thirteen friends for the last quarter so they could graduate with them in 1916, with Ray as salutatorian. What a contrast it must have been to go from the great school at Mount Hermon to the tiny confines of Contoocook!

In many ways the year at Mount Hermon was a crucial turning point in Ray's life. Charles Alexander, the evangelist and musician, associated with D. L. Moody, conducted two weeks of meetings at the school. For Ray this was a spiritual crisis because for some years he had been a Christian, but only a half-hearted one. During Mr. Alexander's meetings, the Holy Spirit worked so thoroughly through Ray's will that he was brought to a life-changing experience of consecration and dedication.

During this year a missionary speaker named Mr. Warner, who had been working in Bolivia, spoke at the school. Ray was stirred as he heard about the needs of that neglected country and the entire continent of South America. In these days when Latin America is thriving spiritually, it is well to remember what a great reversal has taken place. In the great missionary conference in Edinburgh in 1910, South America was not even represented, as there were so few missionaries working there. The continent was considered to be Christian because of the influence of Roman Catholicism, and apparently the thousands of untouched areas were to be ignored. Mr. Warner, then something of a rarity, had a burning message concerning the needs of Latin America. Ray was stirred, and dates his missionary call from that evening. He thought he was destined for South America, although events led him eventually to Burma.

The Student Volunteer Movement was active in those days and to be a member you had to have answered the call for missionary service. The SVM functioned only in colleges and universities; Mount Hermon was the only preparatory school with an SVM chapter. Ray immediately joined, and at the age of seventeen he was clear and determined what his life's vocation was to be: he was to be a missionary.

In the year at Mount Hermon, three developments took place that were to shape his future years. He discovered that he had an aptitude for running, his Christian commitment had become a reality, and he had received a call to missionary service. So much could not have been dreamed of when the two small boys entered the gates of Mount Hermon in 1915.

Mount Hermon had an outstanding Bible teacher on the faculty, an Australian named Dr. J. East Harrison, personally chosen by D. L. Moody. In his fifth term at Mt. Hermon Ray was chosen to be an assistant in the Bible department, but assistants were not required to take courses in that department. Late in his sixth term he realized he was missing one of Mount Hermon's greatest contributions for him, namely, Dr. Harrison's classes. So in the spring term of 1917 he took a postgraduate program, enrolling in courses taught by Dr. Harrison, with an additional Greek course as well, continuing all the while to hone his running skills.

# 2

# COLLEGE YEARS

There were four colleges in the State of Maine: the University of Maine; Bowdoin College (where Henry Longfellow had studied); and two Baptist colleges—Colby which was Calvinistic Baptist and Bates College which was Free Will Baptist.

The twins selected Bates College largely because their father was a Bates graduate and their two older brothers also attended there. It was established in 1870 and was one of the first to be coed. Bates had an enrollment of approximately 600 and was tending to become theologically liberal, especially the religion department. Ray took no religion courses there for he had received a firm foundation in the Word at Mount Hermon and was planning to go to seminary. The college later became thoroughly liberal theologically.

The twins had saved for a year for their college education and continued to work their way through, supplemented by summer jobs. In this they were greatly helped by an aunt, Eva Francis Buker, who was an outstanding person. She had been raised on a farm at Sabattus, Maine, and when she graduated from high school she began to teach in the one-room school in Webster, a few miles from Sabattus. During her early years of teaching she studied German with a tutor and continued her studies in Bavaria, Germany, for a year. She did so well that the combination of her blonde appearance and fluency in German caused the Germans to exclaim, "But Fraulein, you *are* a German." Later she became vice-principal of the Brooklyn Training School for teachers. President Chase of Bates College considered her one of the most astute and able teachers he knew; Bates granted her an honorary M.A. degree although she never attended college. During the time the twins were at college she moved to Lewiston, Maine, so that she could make a home for them. She charged nothing for their room and board, but far more than that, her maturity and breadth of understanding were a constant help to Dick and Ray.

During the summer of 1917 Ray worked at Hampton Beach, New Hampshire, as a dishwasher, and at the Navy Yard at Portsmouth, New Hampshire. Just as he was due to enter Bates he had to have surgery for a hernia, so he had to begin his freshman year six months later than Dick. After recovering from surgery he worked at the Navy Yard again, this time as an apprentice driller. After Mount Hermon the twins took a three-month commercial course where they learned typing skills.

Dick completed his college work in three-and-a-half years, and during this period both he and Ray felt the call to be missionaries. Dick, however, had had a few humiliating experiences in preaching and so concluded that he should be a medical missionary. He therefore took premedical courses.

All this took place after the United States had entered the First World War and there was much confusion. Ray entered the Student Army Training Corp, waited four months for his uniform, and by the time he received it he was discharged because the war was over. He started his freshman year in 1918 and found the uniform to be invaluable as he had no money to buy other clothes.

His views on education were more typical of Europe than of America and he still retains them. He wanted a broad classical education, believing that he could pick up other subjects later on, often by private reading. During his years at college he completed eight years of Greek, and he had a double major in Greek and philosophy. He was also in the Hellenic Club, the Physics Club, and the Spofford Club; all this in addition to the Student Volunteer Movement, the Young Men's Christian Association, and his running. Despite all these extra activities in his junior year he was second in his class scholastically. Because of the war there were no cross-country races in the fall of 1918 when he entered Bates.

In the spring of 1919, in his freshman year, Ray ran in the two-mile event and came in second, and because of this he was entitled to wear a Bates Varsity sweater and letter. During the summer of that year he again worked in the Navy Yard, and later he traveled to North Dakota to help with the wheat harvest. He had heard that he could earn more money doing farm work in North Dakota than he could get in any job in New England. He made his way to Chicago where he discovered he could get a free train ride to North Dakota by working on the railroad. When he got there he obtained work with a farmer in Valley City, North Dakota. Although the pay was good, the work was hard and the days long. Moreover, he had not had the opportunity to gain the skills demonstrated by the local farm laborers. It was fortunate that his superb physical condition plus a lifetime of adapting to differing forms of labor enabled him to cope. However, working on the farm was not without incident. One day a huge threshing machine was brought into the field by a team of horses. Several farmers set their farm hands to forking the wheat into the thresher, while others loaded the carts and drove them and their teams of horses with the grain. Ray was forking the sheaves into the machine. Now, a pitchfork is very long; in fact, it must have been almost as long as Ray was tall. Ray lost his footing and his grip on the fork, which fell into the machine. There was a horrible grinding noise and the machine stopped. A part had broken and the thresher could not be restarted until a new part could be fitted. So the farmer had to go to the nearest town, and during that time a number of farm hands were of necessity idle. You can imagine Ray's feelings, and how surprised he was that he wasn't fired.

Soon after this humiliating experience a team of horses bolted, dragging with them the hay rack. One of the farm hands gave chase, but lacked the speed to overtake the horses. Ray immediately took off after the runaway animals, which by now were heading toward a gate too narrow for the cart to pass through. As Ray anticipated, the man fell and lay spread-eagled on the ground. Ray ran right over him. His right foot fell clear of the man's foot and his left foot just cleared the man's head. Although he was only 5'7" his stride was more than six feet long. He caught up with the hay rack, flung himself on it, and worked his way forward until he could grasp the reins of the horses and bring them under control. He felt he had atoned for the damage to the thresher! The team passed through the fence gate at an angle—a veritable miracle.

This incident gives an insight into Ray's running ability. He had already learned that a runner must run from his hips and not his knees. In his countless hours of training he had watched his shadow as he ran. The successful athlete running from his hips with a long stride could see that the shadow of his head did not bob up and down but glided along in a smooth, level line.

In the fall of 1919 he took part in the Maine State Intercollegiate cross-country. Four colleges took part and the race was held at Colby. Ray won first place; and it was the first time he had taken part in an intercollegiate cross-country race.

In the spring of 1920 both Ray and Dick were invited to take part in the tryouts for the Olympics due to be held that summer in Antwerp. They then learned that the tryouts for the 1500 meters were to be held on Sunday. Their strong conviction concerning Sunday observance led them to decline the invitation. Years later Ray felt that this was a good thing because at that time they had not yet matured sufficiently. However, it may have given them the idea that Ray should attempt to see if he was good enough for the 1924 Olympics. Dick found it necessary to drop out of competitive racing after graduation because of the heavy academic load at medical school, but Ray intended to continue his running through his seminary years.

Ray began his junior year at Bates in the fall of 1920. For the first time since the war the college entered a team for the New England Cross-Country event held in Boston at the Franklin Park course. Ray was a member of that team. It was a strange course, and although it had some gentle slopes it had none of the steep hills that were characteristic of all his cross-country races in Maine. At about a mile from the finish Ray was so far behind the leaders that he was convinced that humanly speaking he could never place, even if he used his sprint for the last part of the race. He prayed, telling the Lord that perhaps it was not His will that he should win, and that he didn't know how he could. The Lord answered, "Start to sprint." Ray replied, "Lord, You know that one can't sprint for a mile." He felt that God's answer entered his soul, "You obey Me and you will see what I can do." Ray began to sprint. He soon drew even with the leaders—and finished first.

In 1921, in the spring of Ray's junior year, Bates decided to compete in the Penn Relays, which had a long history and attracted the best athletes from far and wide. The decision to enter was not easy. Bates had never previously entered a track event outside of New England, and besides that, the Penn Relays were international. The meet was held in Philadelphia, which was a fairly long distance from Lewiston, Maine—especially in those days of slow travel. Another complication was the fact that spring in Maine was late and the track was covered with snow. It was almost impossible to be in peak condition as early as April. In spite of these difficult factors, Ray worked hard in training.

The Penn Relays were a totally new experience for Ray, the country boy. He knew that his only experience in running was with intercollegiate racing in New England, yet as he traveled south to meet national athletes from all over the USA the enormity of the responsibility he bore weighed heavily on his shoulders. Bates was almost unknown outside of New England, and he was a totally unknown athlete. He knew that the most famous intercollegiate two-mile runner was a man named Nightingale from West Virginia, and he hoped he would not be available for the race. When he arrived Ray examined the roster to discover that not only had Nightingale entered but also Furnas of Purdue, also highly regarded. Ray revealed his despondency by writing a post card to Dick saying, "Nightingale is here; all is lost."

The twins had so often been ridiculed in school for being small that it was difficult for them to overcome feelings of inadequacy. Little Ray at 5'7'' certainly felt like a baseball player from a minor league suddenly catapulted into a World Series. It is not difficult to imagine his feelings since all he heard from the crowd was that Nightingale was certain to win the two-mile event. What the crowd saw was a small man with a big heart who knew only one way to run, whatever the competition. He would give the race every ounce of strength he had, for his Lord, his college, and himself.

Ray took his place on a strange track, in an international event, with only two men in the crowd supporting him. The starting pistol sounded and they were off. Nightingale and Furnas soon took the lead and held it. With half a mile to go they were in a life-and-death struggle with Cecil Leath of New Hampshire, with Ray about twenty yards back. The pistol sounded, announcing the fact that the last lap of the race had started. The runners maintained their positions, but four hundred yards from the finish Ray made his bid by turning on his devastating sprint. Soon he was even with Nightingale, who heard him coming and turned around to the left to look; a disastrous thing for a runner of his experience to do. A middle-distance runner would occasionally look over his right shoulder in the earlier stages of a race to see where his competitors were, but when Ray began his final sprint his eyes were riveted only on the finishing tape. Nothing and no one could be allowed to divert his concentration or to break his stride. While Nightingale was turning, Ray flashed past him, and when he turned back to the front Ray was in the lead and drawing away. He was still drawing away when he broke the tape twenty-five yards ahead of his nearest rival. He had run the last quarter in fifty-eight seconds. Ray's time for the entire race was 9.25: a fast race and one good enough to cause a sensation, although it was a record that held for some twenty years.

The press and the crowd were amazed at the upset performance by the little unknown man who had taken everyone by surprise. Nightingale completely dropped out of competitive running and was never heard of again.

The *Boston Globe* ran a large picture of Ray complete with a front-page writeup telling "how this boy from the cow pastures of Maine came down and showed his heels to the world." Tom McCabe of the *Boston Herald* wrote, "The little Bates lad was great, big, fine, wonderful; all those pulsating things together, and then some. Pure grit, from the feet up." The college newspaper, the *Bates Student,* was understandably even more exuberant in its report.

> "The little Bates lad was great, big, fine, wonderful; all those pulsating things together, and then some. Pure grit, from the feet up, he headed a field of New England beauties." Such is the manner in which Tom McCabe, the feature editor of athletics in the *Boston Herald,* describes Ray Buker, after his wonderful exhibition at the Penn relay carnival last Friday afternoon. But those words can serve only to stir up anew the joyful sensations felt by all as the bell on Hathorn Hall pealed out the message that the lad whom we had sent to represent the Garnet at

Pennsylvania had won a glorious victory over the best distance runners of America. After all, words are feeble, for no use of them has yet been able to picture the inward emotions we feel, when someone to whom we have allotted a most difficult task has accomplished it in a manner that is nothing short of marvelous. As the bell sounded the joyful news, our first impulse was that quiet, deep, stirring of the inner man that sends lumps into the throats and renders us unable to speak. Then comes the rush of pride for our champion and the pent-up emotions spring into a hilarious burst of enthusiasm and gratitude for the man who has brought us fame. Such were the feelings of every Bates man and woman last Friday night. Ray has brought an outstanding honor to our Alma Mater, an honor which is nation-wide and for which we are greatly indebted to him.

Tom McCabe called it "Yankee pluck," but something way beyond that actuated the splendid lad in giving to us all the wonderful ability which he possesses. A steadfast purpose of bringing glory to Bates spurred him on. It surely took a great deal of some very high quality of courage for Buker to compete in the Penn games. These constitute the one big athletic carnival of the year and contestants of the highest reputation assemble and strive for the prestige which comes by winning a coveted first place. For weeks prior to the carnival the press had heralded such men as Nightingale of West Virginia, Furnas, the Purdue star, and Cecil Leath of New Hampshire State. Little did they foresee that a lad from "Bates College, way up in Lewiston, Me., uncalled, unheralded, yes, even as late as the last lap of the big international two-mile race, unsuspected of any evil intent on a champion's crown," had to be reckoned with. They had their winner picked and he was invincible. But the warm sun shone down on the great event and smiled as those champions of the past were outclassed and outdistanced by the fleet little youth from Bates. "Dirigo" the motto of the State of Maine was personified in one of her collegians.

And such a race as it must have been for those privileged to witness it! Practically unknown by the vast crowd of people attending and with only a couple of fellow students eagerly watching from the stands, Ray fought against great odds. The starting pistol sounded and the grind was on. The favored contestants dashed off full of confidence; Buker was way back in a group of 20-odd starters. The mighty Nightingale and Furnas took things easy until the end of the first mile and then they led the field, with the former man slightly ahead of the Purdue runner. Then the last half mile came and found these same two competitors in a life and death struggle. Leath of New Hampshire State was pressing close to them but Buker was 20 yards back and not giving the checkers any cause for worriment. The pistol sounded again, this time to announce that a single lap remained, the one in which every drop of energy must be sacrificed. Still the three leaders held their respective places and the crowd was satisfied who the winner was to be. As they neared the last 300 yards the unexpected happened. Buker shot out of the bunch in which he had been traveling and started that deadly spurt of his. The spectators began to realize that something was happening. They burst into cheers as the plucky lad tore by his opponents. The Furnas fire went out; the Nightingale drooped his feathers, a defeated star. The Bates champion had crossed the line 25 yards ahead of his nearest man. Raymond Buker had brought fame to himself and honor and distinction to the college which he represented. All honor to our champion!

Ray was immediately catapulted to fame. He was to dominate the one- and two-mile events for years, and in addition put Bates on the map as far as track was concerned.

In the fall of 1921, his senior year, following a summer missionary pastorate in Aroostook, Maine, he entered the Maine Intercollegiate cross-country event held at the University of Maine. On the morning of the event four inches of sleet fell, making the course very difficult for the athletes. One and a half miles from the finish line, while he was in the lead, Ray lost a shoe. He had to make a lightning quick decision: if he stopped to replace the shoe he might be passed and have the psychological difficulty of trying to recapture the lead. On the other hand, ahead was a treacherous stretch of the course named "Standpipe Hill." It had a surface of shale rock and at the end of the race was one lap on a cinder track. But Ray did not hesitate: he endured the pain and finished the race in first place by half a lap. The achievement caused a sensation.

One evening in the winter of 1921 Dick, Ray, and their brother Gerald were sitting in the home of their Aunt Eva studying.

Gerald suggested, "Let's go down to Ross's and have some ice cream."

"No you don't, that would break Ray's diet, and he is going to be in the Olympics in 1924," said Dick.

Ray had a lifelong love of ice cream and Ross's in Lewiston was well known for good ice cream and was therefore a favorite place of students from Bates, so Ray leaped to Gerald's suggestion.

"Dick, be reasonable, the Olympics are three years away," argued Ray.

"You are not going," ordered Dick.

"Try to stop me," replied Ray and darted through the door. Like a flash Dick was after him. Ray sprinted down the road. After four blocks Dick caught him and a rueful Ray was dragged back home.

"Dick has never beaten me in a race but that night he caught me in four blocks."

In the spring of his senior year Ray again entered the Penn Relays. But this year it was different. Instead of being the little "unknown" he was now accepted as a middle distance runner. No one dared challenge him; he would take the lead for a short time and then slow down, but the other runners would also slow down so he would be in the lead again. It was a very easy race for him and no challenge. When the runners came to the last lap he did not slow down but sprinted as he usually did. He did not overexert himself. His time was ten seconds slower than the previous year but he had won, and that was all that mattered.

That same spring he also ran in the National Collegiate Athletic Association two-mile race at Harvard Stadium. He touched the ribbon in a dead tie, as evidenced by a photo record, but the judges awarded him second place.

As Ray came to the end of his college days in 1922 he thought it was time to take inventory. Athletically he had progressed every year until he was now a force to be reckoned with. He was famous for his awesome finishing sprint. He had practiced a training method for years and had now perfected it. He had also developed strong views about the ideal racing diet. The diet consisted of no cake and a moderate amount of milk; he had discovered that too much milk could slow him down. He ate lots of vegetables and fruit, but little meat. He had learned from an experiment carried out at Yale. One group of students was fed a lot of meat; the other group was put on a vegetarian diet. After many weeks they were tested as to their endurance. Among other tests they were made to stand and extend their arms out from their shoulders. The meat eaters held their arms out for fifteen minutes; the vegetarians for *two hours and fifteen minutes.* This lesson was then compared to the animal kingdom. The meat eaters, such as lions, had sudden violent strength, but it was found that elephants and bovine creatures that were vegetarians had great endurance. As a distance runner Ray knew that his great need was for endurance and he planned his diet accordingly. Although his diet was tailored for successful running, it also had the advantage of being economical. The Olympics were scheduled for 1924. Ray set his goal on running in them. Not only would he run for himself and his country, but it would also give him the opportunity for a long desired trip to Europe.

Academically he had proved to be an excellent student and had received a classical education that was to provide a solid foundation for the rest of his life. In his senior year Ray studied New Testament Greek, the easiest of the eight years of Greek he took. However, at the end of the year his Greek professor insisted on giving him a "B" instead of an "A," not because he lacked the requisite knowledge, but because he had missed class time to participate in track events. Because of this professor's action Ray just missed receiving a Phi Beta Kappa Key. He was heartbroken. The other members of the faculty were very reasonable about his missing classes, and when Ray told his geology professor that he would gladly give up all his athletic medals and awards to get his Phi Beta Kappa, the professor admitted that if they had been aware of this earlier some special arrangement could possibly have been worked out. Dick still feels that Ray was cheated.

Ray had also matured spiritually, and before the academic year finished he visited every athlete in his room to press on him the claims of Jesus Christ. Not one responded. From a missionary viewpoint his knowledge had broadened and his conviction of his call had deepened; a conviction that never wavered.

There were four or five black students at Bates and Ray was a close friend of two of them. One, Benjamin E. Mays, was an outstanding debater. When Oxford University sent a debating team to Bates, Mays was not allowed to take part because he was black. This was ironic because if he had been an undergraduate at Oxford he would have been permitted to participate. He was also refused a Phi Beta Kappa, and Ray was incensed at these injustices. Benny Mays eventually received 21 honorary degrees and 200 citations, and became the President of Moorehouse College and a frequent advisor to President Kennedy. In later years Bates gave him two honorary doctorates and his Delta Sigma Rho and Phi Beta Kappa. Ray has always hated racial discrimination, and when he married he chose a black friend as best man at his wedding.

When Ray graduated from college he was unfailingly friendly, very genial, slow to disagree, with a marked sense of humor. This surface appearance tended to cover up the fact that he held many principles very deeply and continued to hold them with the same doggedness he displayed on the track.

Dorothy was a year behind Ray in college. During his senior year they became engaged with the understanding that they would marry following her graduation.

The college yearbook summed up Ray's college years as follows:

Raymond Bates Buker '22

Freshman Prize Debate
Varsity Track 1,2,3,4
Varsity Cross Country 2,3,4
Captain, Track & Cross Country 4
Politics Club, Treasurer 4
Phil-Hellenic Club
Jordan Scientific Society
Class Chaplain 1,2,3,4
Leader, Student Volunteer Group 4
President, YMCA 4

"The little Bates man was wonderful, marvelous, courageous, pulsating—all these things and more as he passed the last man and sprinted, a winner, to the tape." That's how a Boston writer described Ray's shattering of the two-mile mark. Bates is proud—and lucky—to have as a track captain an international champion.

This is the first concrete evidence that Ray had an incredible range of interests. Moreover, bearing in mind the large number of hours he spent weekly in athletic training and competition, his academic record revealed the fact that he had a brilliant mind.

The Buker family about 1913. Raymond is standing at the far right. His twin, Richard, is sitting on the floor.

As a student at Mount Hermon in 1917.

As a member of Bates Cross-Country team.

The 1919 Bates Cross-Country team. Raymond is second from the left and Richard is third from the right.

Raymond, Dorothy, and Raymond, Jr. just before going to Burma in 1926.

# 3

# SEMINARY YEARS

During his college years Ray had avoided taking courses in the Department of Religion because it was liberal in its theology, and also because he believed he already had a good biblical foundation, laid first at home and then at Mount Hermon. At college he was often accused of having a closed mind. He was also told that the reason he held conservative theological convictions was that he had never exposed himself to other viewpoints, and perhaps there was some truth in these assertions. But later, as he was obligated to take part in some controversies, he proved he was not ignorant of liberal positions. No one could question his excellent academic ability. Some said that as he had led a protected life he should attend an "enlightened seminary" where the "truth" was taught. He asked where such an institution existed and was told that the University of Chicago Divinity School was such a place.

Ray gave the suggestion much thought and prayer. There were dangers involved in a liberal seminary as he well knew, but there were also some advantages. He planned to spend his life as a missionary with the American Baptist Foreign Mission Society where he would often come into contact with people of liberal theological persuasion, so he felt it would greatly strengthen his position if his credentials included study in liberal institutions. Furthermore, he would be in a better position to refute those liberal ideas if he had studied them in depth. There were two other considerations. First, the University of Chicago had a professor from Bolivia, South America, and Ray still felt that his missionary call was to South America. Professors from that neglected continent were rare in 1922. Also, he could take his master's degree in missions in one year, so Ray decided to go to Chicago. And it proved to be a grim experience. It was one of the darkest years in his life.

To attend the divinity school he had to leave Dick and the rest of his family and friends, and for the first time he had to live in a huge, impersonal city. He missed the steep hills and beautiful scenery of his native Maine. The bleak, cold city with long winters, where the fall was brief and spring even briefer, held no attraction for a boy brought up in the country. He was lonely, but he gritted his teeth and carried on doggedly.

Added to the unpleasant climate was the character of the divinity school. Here he discovered a liberal theology that taught a religion with no personal God and a soulless man. He found an example of liberalism that itself had a closed mind to the views of others, and where openness of mind was a mockery. The missions professor summed up the attitude of the whole school when he stubbornly insisted, "You can pray till you are blue in the face and it will do you no good." It was a tough time for Ray.

One or two incidents illustrate the school's viewpoint. The Old Testament professor gave an assignment on "The Concept of Sin in the Book of Isaiah." Ray studied the book carefully and then used a concordance to make a list of every place where sin is mentioned. Based on this research he wrote his paper. It was returned with the grade "C−," and the comment. "This is a crazy patchwork quilt. I will give you a passing grade because you worked hard."

On another occasion the same professor, J. M. P. Smith, in referring to 1 Kings 19, commented that if Elijah had walked backwards it would not have taken forty days and nights to reach Horeb. Only once while attending the divinity school in Chicago did Ray raise his hand and interject a comment. It was here, and he said that "although he was no Hebrew scholar, the English rendering seemed to emphasize not that it took forty days and nights to reach Horeb, but rather that the food and water provided Elijah with the strength to last for forty days and nights." There was utter silence in the room; the professor gave him a scornful glare and continued his lecture with no mention of Ray's opinion. Ray met only close-minded prejudice.

It seemed that the best way to get good grades was to skim the book to be studied and then put it away and write a creative essay out of your head, using little biblical content. The professors did not appreciate anything that made the Bible central. Though Ray often felt battered by impersonal humanistic lectures, he held his own by determined and exhaustive studies in the divinity school library and by long talks with President Taft of the Northern Baptist Theological Seminary. Most of all, his faith was sustained by his own devotional life. It was a spiritual parallel to the stubborn persistence that had helped him overcome the obstacles of track and still emerge a winner. It was to be characteristic of his entire life.

His athletic activities were a welcome contrast during this period of his life. As he was no longer an undergraduate, he was to race under the auspices of the American Athletic Union. As a graduate student he could not belong to the varsity team, so he joined the Illinois Athletic Club. He trained under Tom Eck who did much to perfect his running skills. He trained very hard on an indoor track and enjoyed his first perfect season, winning every race he entered, all in Chicago. But in March 1923, he took part in an important and well-known race, the Banker's Mile; and once again he came in first. The final race of the regular season was a two-mile event. The favorite for the race was Joey Ray, who also trained under Tom Eck and who had enjoyed a brilliant season. Since the race was the last of the day, many people had left, assuming that Joey Ray was bound to win. There were twelve laps to the race, and four or five laps from the finish Ray passed Joey Ray to take the lead. Joey was astonished, and at the next straightaway he passed Ray. Then at the next straightaway, Ray passed him again and so it continued. With two laps to go Ray turned on his sprint, took the lead, and kept it to the tape. The spectators and press declared it the most exciting race they had seen in years. Joey Ray never beat Ray Buker.

The academic year culminated in an incredibly busy and important week in June 1923. After Ray completed his studies for his master's degree, he traveled by train from Chicago to Lewiston, Maine. While there two significant events took place: his future father-in-law took him to Dorothy's hometown, North Baldwin, Maine, to obtain a marriage license, and he was ordained to the gospel ministry. Shortly after that he took a train back to Chicago for a special relay race that had been planned; the Illinois Athletic Club had four outstanding mile runners at that time and it was decided that they should attack the world record for the four-mile relay race.

There was no competition. The race was really against the clock. It took place on a Chicago track on June 23, 1923, with the temperature at 100°F, and with typical Chicago humidity. The first runner in the relay was Egil Krogh who ran his mile in 4:28.8; the second was Ray Buker who ran his leg of the race in 4:20.9. Ray Watson, a one-handed runner, clocked the excellent time of 4:12.4, close to the world record. Joey Ray anchored the race with the time of 4:16.6. The overall time was 17:21.4, breaking the world record by 23 seconds, and this record was to stand for more than twenty years. Each member of the team was awarded a miniature running shoe made of gold with a small diamond in the toe. The time of the race, 17:21, was engraved on the sole of each shoe. Mrs. Buker wore this trophy proudly on a chain as a necklace.

On June 27, 1923, Ray and Dorothy were married, with one of Ray's black friends from college, Theodore Roosevelt Pinkney, as best man. In choosing him Ray gave public recognition of his deeply felt conviction that the pigment of a man's skin was not half so important as the person himself.

The wedding took place in Dorothy's hometown of North Baldwin, preceded by a most unusual event. The water for the home at North Baldwin was supplied by a spring and that very morning, to the consternation of all, a dog had fallen in. Ray and his best man spent a frantic hour or two bailing out the polluted water. Unfortunately, Dick found it necessary to be absent from Ray's wedding owing to lack of funds for travel; and interestingly enough, when Dick was married the following September, Ray couldn't attend because of the same problem. Ray and Dorothy spent their honeymoon traveling to Hickory, Virginia, where happy days were enjoyed in the home of Ray's oldest brother, Harold.

In the fall of 1923 Ray enrolled at Oberlin Divinity School, where he and Dorothy rented a cozy second-floor apartment. The landlord and his wife were a warm Christian couple who were extremely kind to them, and Ray later described this year as "one of the happiest years of our life."

The atmosphere in the Oberlin Divinity School was in sharp contrast to that of the University of Chicago Divinity School. Even though the school was liberal in its theology by this time, Dean Graham and President Bosworth saw to it that everyone was treated with kindness and tolerance, whatever views they held. Early in the academic year, when Ray took a course in "The Philosophy of Religion," the class was assigned to write a paper on the subject, "Why was William Jennings Bryan wrong?" This paper gave Ray his first opportunity to express himself. He gave much thought to the subject and eventually wrote a paper on, "Why was William Jennings Bryan *right?*" When the graded papers were handed back he found to his great surprise he had been given an "A." A greater surprise followed. Professor Youtz announced to the class, "We teach a method of study and one paper submitted illustrates that method. I do not share the views of Mr. Buker but he has demonstrated his grasp of the study method. Mr. Buker, will you please read your paper to the class?"

At Oberlin he found liberalism, but a totally different kind from that of the University of Chicago. Oberlin represented a liberal theology with an open mind and a personal God, and under these conditions Ray thrived. The tolerance was as true of the students as of the faculty.

In the fall of 1923 Ray began coaching Oberlin's cross-country team on an amateur basis. He needed more men on the team, and he knew one student who was capable—Ernie Edmonds of New Zealand, a former soccer star. Ray went to his room to persuade him to join, and he promised Ernie that the daily practice period would not last more than half an hour. He encouraged him by saying that it would so clear his mind that he would accomplish more studying in two hours than he could normally do in three.

The next spring the Olympics were to be held in Paris. Ray had his mind set on being a member of the American team, and seized every opportunity to prepare himself for this great event. He trained hard and successfully won every track event he entered, prior to the tryouts held at Harvard in June.

In preparing the cross-country team Ray used to spend the first five minutes giving instructions on some aspect of training or running. At their last session he spoke to them about prayer, and stressed from his own long experience the fact that prayer could and should have a vital role in competition. On Easter Sunday they were staying in a hotel in a city in Iowa where they had raced the day before. As Ray was preparing to go to church that morning he was pleasantly surprised when every one of his teammates appeared in his room and announced that they were going to church with him. It was their way of expressing their esteem for Ray and the principles he so faithfully held and practiced.

At the end of the 1924 academic year Dorothy traveled back to Maine, and Ray went to Chicago for a period of final training from Tom Eck in preparation for the Olympic trials. He also ran in various regional elimination events, and since he was still a member of the Illinois Athletic Club, he wore the club's tricolor when he raced.

The Olympic tryouts took place in June and attracted not only the top athletes in the nation, but also widespread press coverage. The Boston newspapers were filled with daily reports of the events and of the arrival of different athletes every day. The tension and excitement almost reached a frenzy as the week progressed. The heats of the 1500 meters were to be held on Friday with the final on Saturday. You can imagine that Ray was under growing tension and for him the week seemed more like a month. He planned his tactics with meticulous care because he wanted to be in the peak of condition for the Saturday finals. He decided that in the heats he would not go all out but only run fast enough to be certain of getting into the finals.

Ray had not been beaten that year but he did not permit himself to be overconfident. He knew the best runners were there so he would use the Friday heats to calmly estimate the potential of his rivals; but his plans were shattered when the heats were cancelled, and this meant that all the 1500-meter runners were to fight it out on Saturday. Ray spent Friday resting and reviewing his tactics for the finals. He knew that the Boston College men, coached by Jack Ryan, would go all out at the start hoping to get so far in the lead they could not be caught. Ray as usual would hold himself in check at the beginning and rely on his final sprint to win the race.

Saturday, the final day of the trials dawned and the 1500 meters was to be the big event of the day. One can imagine the tension that mounted as the day wore on, and it inevitably affected Ray. His old teammate, Joey Ray, had undergone a tonsillectomy and thus would not be competing in the 1500 meters but would be watching from the sidelines. Ray Buker knew this, but strangely the press did not, and all that week they ran stories speculating on the final showdown by these friendly rivals.

At last the time of the race arrived and all the athletes took their places. The starting pistol cracked and they were off. As Ray anticipated, the Boston College men raced to an early lead, faster than even Ray expected. They were clocked at fifty-six seconds for the first quarter, a grueling pace. It was long before sophisticated timing, but Ray had learned to time himself to a second, by the muscles in his crotch. He knew that he was doing the first quarter at fifty-nine to sixty seconds, exactly what he had planned. By this time the Boston College men were in the lead by thirty yards. It was a great temptation to try to catch up, but Ray was not lured. He always ran with his head as well as his legs.

The race was about three and three-quarters laps. Round the runners went—once, twice, three times. There was just the three-quarters of a lap left. Ray was about twentieth in the pack. Would it be too late? Joey Ray was watching intently on the sidelines, and he heard someone ask, "Hey, where is your teammate Buker? I thought you said he was going to win?"

"Just wait, the race is not over yet," replied Joey, reflecting an optimism that he probably did not feel at the moment. Finally one curve and the last straightaway remained. Ray began his awesome sprint and soon shot out of the pack with his great stride and burst of speed—taking the lead. Lloyd Hahn, an old and friendly rival, said to himself, "There goes Ray; I must follow." Spencer, a runner from Mississippi whose coach had given him one word of instruction, "Follow Buker," sprinted past Ray, thinking to himself, "I may not win the race, but I will at least have a chance to place."

As Ray entered the final turn, in astonishment he said to himself, "Who is this fellow? I am doing my best. Is there a man in America who can beat me? Either he'll fade or prove his ability as the winner." He did indeed fade. Ray passed him on the final straightaway and came in first by a comfortable margin with Lloyd Hahn second, Spencer third, and Connally fourth. These men would represent the US in the Olympics.

Pandemonium broke out in the stands at this exciting finish. Ray's time was 3.55, *equalling the American record.* The time for the 1500 meter would be equivalent to 4.06 for the mile.

In the past few years scores of expert athletes have been asked what they thought would have been the best time for the mile in 1924. Their estimates have ranged from 4.25 to 4.15; all have been astonished at Ray's time, and Ray regards it as the best race he ever ran. The four-minute mile was not broken until twenty years later in 1954 when it was accomplished by Roger Bannister, now Sir Roger, a distinguished neurosurgeon. This race gives us a good idea of Ray's ability at the height of his running career.

After the sensational display at Boston Ray was an automatic choice for the Olympic Games for which he had prepared so many years. The American Olympic organizers knew from long experience that their middle-distance runners had never performed well in European events but they did nothing to correct their mistakes. The trials were held late. This did not allow sufficient time for adequate preparation for the actual event which was due to start on Bastille Day, July 14, in Paris.

This left only a month for the journey to France in addition to many essential preparations. There were countless matters to be taken care of before Ray left for the slow voyage across the Atlantic; and the all-important on-the-spot training to hone the skills to the standard required for Olympic competition.

Success for Ray had always depended on years of the most rigid self-disciplined training and meticulous planning. It was particularly frustrating to realize that his laboriously acquired edge was draining away on the slow journey across the Atlantic. He did everything he could to keep in condition, including jogging and calisthenics. However, he knew that there was no substitute for daily on-the-track training. He was determined to do everything he could to train extra hard when they arrived in Paris. Alas, it was not to be.

After their arrival they were housed in dismal wooden huts in a military camp far from the practice track. Ray found that he was spending more time sitting in buses traveling to the practice site than running on the track! Perhaps the most disgraceful thing was that the coaches on whom they so greatly depended did nothing to help, but spent their time exploring the night life of Paris. Their expenses had been paid by the American Olympic organizers, and such callous disregard of their duties would be ruthlessly exposed by the media if it occurred in our day. Ray would have given anything to have had the advice of John Eck, his personal coach, but he was still in Chicago.

Although Ray had traveled fairly extensively in the United States it was the first time he had been in another country. The circumstances were such that just when he needed to be physically and mentally as sharp as a razor he was almost totally disoriented and bewildered by the babel of the different languages to which he was subjected.

He had no illusions concerning the quality of the men he would be competing against. Each country was permitted to send four men, and naturally they sent the cream of their athletes. Much to his surprise Ray found that his reputation had preceded him. His competitors took every opportunity to assess the American champion.

All too soon Bastille Day dawned and the opening ceremonies of the games took place. The American contingent numbered three or four hundred from every sport. The opening parade was impressive with the arrival of the Olympic torch and the lighting of the eternal flame. When asked if he was emotionally stirred by all this pageantry, Ray replied quickly, "I was always proud of being an American." Then he added more slowly, "No, I felt no particular emotion; I had studied the Greeks, their history, culture, and literature for so long that I knew that this was a very superficial replica of the real thing. I wished I could have used that time for extra practice. I knew I was running for the honor of my country and I felt depressed that I was not in shape to do justice for such a great responsibility."

As Ray examined the list of competitors in the 1500 meters he knew that the greatest threat was Nurmi of Finland, called the "Flying Fin."

The first question in Ray's mind was whether he would even get through the heats and into the finals. The competition was fierce, and Ray did his utmost to plan his strategy to make the most of the situation. He was far more at home running the mile than the 1500 meters, but he had more serious problems. In planning his races in the United States with Tom Eck he knew that his best strategy was to aim at covering each quarter of a mile in fifty-eight to fifty-nine seconds. This allowed him to reserve enough strength for his blistering sprint that had won so many races for him. In France, surrounded by strange languages, and out of condition, he could not even find anyone who would hold a stop watch for him!

The first four in each heat would be in the final 1500 meters. In his heat he was the only American, and he dare not overextend himself in his condition. The heat took place and despite the quality of the competition he found that even by trying to use it as another training session he was doing well. However, he contented himself with second place, good enough to put him in the finals but well within his strength.

The closing day of the Games dawned, and the bus journey, which he shared with his friend and rival Lloyd Hahn, seemed endless. Then came the torturous hours of waiting, enlivened by one incident that was indelibly etched upon his memory. One of the competitors for the 1500 meters was Eric Little from Scotland. The Scots have always been strict in the matter of Lord's Day observance and Eric Little was a man of strong Christian convictions. Because his heat was due to be run on a Sunday he withdrew and entered the 440 meters instead. When the final of that event took place, he not only finished first but shattered the world record. Ray joined the enormous roar of enthusiasm as the crowd applauded.

When Little returned to Scotland he was given a hero's welcome. It was difficult to find halls large enough to seat the crowds that thronged to hear him preach the gospel. He eventually joined the China Inland Mission. He and Ray were the only two participants in the 1924 Olympics who became missionaries. Ray kept in touch with Little and by an interesting coincidence they both worked in China. In World War II Ray had a hairbreadth escape from the Japanese. Eric Little was not so fortunate, and died in one of the notorious Japanese concentration camps.

The time eventually came for Ray to make his way to the track and he quietly looked at his rivals. There was the outstanding Nurmi, who despite his poor English was friendly; Lloyd Hahn, his friend from America; two rather haughty medical students from England; and many more who were unknown to him.

It was a pleasant, warm day as they lined up for the start. Soon came the crack of the starter's pistol, and they were off. Round and round they went. At about the three-quarter mark Ray saw Nurmi and one other man in front of him. He had been in much worse positions than this. Then much to his astonishment the two Englishmen passed him with loose running shorts flopping. Soon it was time for the final effort as Ray went into his sprint. For the only time in his life he just lacked the stamina, even though he strained every nerve. The result was, first Nurmi, second Martin (Switzerland), third Stallard (England), fourth Lowe (England), fifth Buker (United States), sixth Hahn (United States). In those days the first six received gold medals so Ray was placed and received his medal.

It is worth noting that the first four had to make only short trips to France. Of all the participants who had traveled great distances, Buker was the first to cross the finishing line. Even then he was not given his time for the race, and he does not know how it compared with his 3.55 in the tryouts.

One thing is certain. He made an impression on an expert. When Nurmi visited the United States three months later the reporter who met him asked if there was an American runner he was afraid of. At once he replied, "Yes, Buker. I saw him run at the Olympics when he was out of condition; I can only imagine how good he must be when he is really at his best."

When the games ended Ray was disappointed that he had not come in first but he had some real compensations. He had given of his best, had been placed, and earned a gold medal, and the United States had won the games. There was one dividend that was even better. All his life Ray had wanted to visit Europe to examine its vast storehouse of treasures of history and art. It had seemed an impossible ambition for a poor country lad, but now his dream came true, and he took full advantage of his opportunity.

France was still recovering from the terrible destruction of World War I, and Ray saw the millions of graves in the military cemeteries. He had missed that war by only a few months. Among the many memorable adventures that he had in Europe was the climbing of the Eiffel Tower, walking up and down the fashionable avenue Champs Élysées. He stood at the Arc de Triumphe and the "Tomb of the Unknown Soldier." Above all he spent what little time and money he could spare to examine the treasures of history and beauty.

Half a day was spent exploring the spectacular wonders of Versailles. Among the cathedrals visited was Nortre Dame and he was enthralled by the Chartres Cathredal dating back to the thirteenth century. He had planned to visit Dresden, the jewel-like capital of Saxony in Germany, but unfortunately his money had run out. Alas, the opportunity was lost forever because that magnificent city was totally destroyed needlessly by Allied Air Forces in February 1945.

Ray was also able to visit the famous art gallery of Louvre which he had longed to explore for years. He eventually discovered the renowned Mona Lisa and even as he stood drinking in its almost mystical attraction he was rudely brought down to earth by the words, "Why are you looking at that junk?" The question came from one of his American Olympic teammates. Patiently Ray tried to explain, but they were on entirely different wavelengths.

He had the company of Lloyd Hahn on some of these expeditions. On the track they were rivals but they had great respect for each other and were excellent companions.

Ray continued his training to prepare for track meets that were to take place in Great Britain, and he was able to get back into peak condition. The United States team traveled from France to London for a meet between the British Empire and the United States.

The day they arrived in London his teammates decided to see a movie. For Ray this seemed a waste of time as there were many places he wanted to visit and he realized that he may never again have the opportunity to visit London. He was not at all interested in royalty so he did not bother to see some of the usual tourist attractions such as Buckingham Palace and St. James's Palace. However, he did visit the National Gallery in Trafalgar Square and reveled in the wonderful paintings on display. He also visited the Tower of London, Westminster Abbey, and St. Paul's Cathedral (built by Sir Christopher Wren). The blue plaques that abound in London fascinated him more than anything else. These gave brief historic notes such as, "In this house Samuel Johnson lived from 1737 to 1739." Another that especially interested him was in Aldersgate Street that stated, "In a room on this site John Wesley was present on May 24, 1738 when a man read from Luther's preface to Romans, and Wesley noted, 'My heart was strangely warmed within me. Then it pleased God to kindle a fire which I trust shall never be extinguished.'"

One of these meets in England was held in the White City stadium in London, between the American track team and the English team. Here he met some of the runners against whom he had raced in France, but it was unfortunate that no 1500-meter or one-mile races were scheduled, thereby denying Ray opportunity to race against Stallard and Lowe, who both finished ahead of him in the Olympics. There was a four-mile relay race in which he took part, and the Americans won comfortably. It is interesting that many years later he was to meet Stallard in Burma, serving as a surgeon at Rangoon City Hospital.

While they were in London the United States team were the guests of a banquet given by the Prince of Wales (later to become the Duke of Windsor). Many of the uninhibited Americans mobbed the Prince, thrusting their menus at him and asking, "Say Prince, will you autograph this?" Although the Prince of Wales seemed amused, Ray was embarrassed as he felt this was a display of bad manners on the part of his countrymen.

From London the team traveled to Glasgow and Ray took part in a one-mile race, a handicap event. Because it was a handicap event (or scratch) in a field of 125 runners, he had the unique experience of seeing 122 competitors drop out of the race one by one as he passed them. His handicap was too great however, and he finished third.

Going on to Dublin, Ray and some members of the American team were invited to take part in a track meet which was supposed to be an Irish Olympic game. Ray had no difficulty in winning.

Following the meet in Dublin the team returned home. Ray was given a first-class ticket, but with his usual economic carefulness he exchanged it for steerage class. With the money he saved, he bought a blue serge suit and an overcoat that he used for the next eight years.

Following Ray's return to the United States, the American Athletic Union held their annual meet in New Jersey. It tended to be anticlimactic after the excitement of the summer, but Ray took part in the mile race and won. He thus became the national one-mile champion of the United States.

He had naturally given much thought as to how he would spend his third and final seminary year. Oberlin held many attractions, and he and Dorothy had been happy there. But even though Ray had a marked sense of humor, he almost seemed at times afraid that too much happiness might make him soft at the very time he was planning a tough and demanding career. Even more important was the realization that in the past he had enjoyed opportunities for cultivation of friendships in rural communities and in the academic community, but he lacked knowledge of work among the needy in the city slums. Therefore, after thinking it all out, he transferred to Boston University School of Theology and arranged to do regular field work in the inner city at Ruggles Street Baptist Church. Here he assisted the Reverend H. J. Thompson as youth pastor. The *Boston Post* wrote this up and announced that Ray would "teach and train the young men of the parish three nights a week and endeavor to steer them right in clean living, as well as make good athletes of them. Ray strongly believes that there is nothing like the athletic life to keep a young fellow in the straight and narrow path. Reverend Buker is an athlete of exceptional ability. If any one were asked to name the great mile runners in the country, yes, in the world, Mr. Buker's name would have to be included with the world's greatest. . . . This reverend gentleman is now a full fledged member of the cloth. With him religion is first—athletics secondary." While Ray may not have used the same phraseology, it is a fair description of his attainments and goals.

The newspaper went on to report, "At the Olympic trials at the Stadium . . . Ray Buker easily showed his class over all American mile runners. . . . He ran one of the most memorable 1500 meters, winning handily, and won in fast time, over one of the greatest fields that ever contested in a 1500 meter event."

Ray always believed that he had gotten the best out of his seminary years. Oberlin had been a happy time and Dorothy and he were able to enjoy weekly concerts given by the famous Oberlin Conservatory of Music. He also felt he had learned much from the professor of church history. He wanted breadth in his seminary training and he certainly obtained it. Boston University School of Theology was often called the School of the Prophets. It placed great emphasis on practical work, and Ray excelled in that. His sense of humor, his compassion for the individual, and of course his Olympic reputation helped him to rapidly win a place in the hearts of the young people.

The warm attitude of this Methodist school appealed to Ray, and he once described himself as a "barnyard existentialist" because he greatly approved of learning from experience, and putting learning into practice. While he was in Boston, Dorothy worked as a city missionary from the Shawnut Avenue Congregational Church.

That year Ray was too busy with his studies and practical work to race in the indoor season, but he did keep in training and left Boston one week before graduation in order to train in Chicago for two weeks preparing himself to defend his title as National American Athletic Union one-mile champion at the NAAU games to be held in San Francisco.

Because he had not taken part in the indoor season it was widely assumed that he had retired from competitive running and the person most likely to win was Lloyd Hahn, who had so often raced against Ray but had never beaten him. Lloyd and Ray were good friends but he naturally thought that perhaps his opportunity had come to win and he could therefore become the American champion at last. Lloyd traveled by railroad to San Francisco and it was not until he bought a newspaper in Denver that he learned that Ray Buker, his old nemesis, would be taking part. You can imagine the psychological shock.

Meanwhile, Ray arranged to arrive in San Francisco with time to spare so that he could hone his conditioning to a fine edge and also could become familiar with a strange track. He learned that the race would be run in the late afternoon, so he practiced every day at that same time. He immediately discovered that every afternoon a strong wind would spring up. Since he was much shorter than the other competitors he thought that this would give him an advantage, so he reasoned that if he by a special "wind stride" could incline his trunk forward slightly, without limiting his stride, he could accentuate that advantage. Lloyd led for 3-1/2 laps but when Ray, going into his wind-stride, crept up on Hahn, Lloyd faded, thus enabling Ray to retain the AAU championship another year. It was only after Ray retired that Hahn became the AAU mile champion. Following this race Ray hung up his track shoes as far as competitive running was concerned. He had started as an undersized unknown boy in Maine, and for nine years, through spartan training and strict diet, had risen until he dominated the one-mile event.

His success was bought at a great price. Often after racing he would throw up until midnight. He prayed about this, "Lord, if all this discipline and suffering are just for my fame, I have already had more than enough." He always felt that the answer was that he should continue solely for the glory of God. Of course, it was immensely invaluable in increasing his large range of interests as demonstrated in his visit to Europe. It also helped prepare him for missionary work in the rugged mountains of Burma and Yunnan, the countries that eventually became his particular field of service.

Although he benefited from training in liberal seminaries, he later saw heartbreaking cases of people he knew and loved being led astray during their studies in such schools. He became convinced that though it had been right for him, he would not recommend it to others. Many years later, when his son chose a seminary, it was a thoroughly conservative one.

# 4

# THEOLOGICAL BACKGROUND

If we are to understand the lives and ministry of the Buker twins, and particularly Ray's, it is essential that we have some idea of the theological climate in which they lived and worked. As early as 1918, when Ray entered Bates College, he was fully aware that the Department of Religion at the school was basically liberal in its theological outlook. Richard took premedical courses, so he did not take any religion courses at Bates. Ray believed that he already had received a thorough foundation in Bible and theology at home and at Mount Hermon; therefore he majored in classics, taking no religion courses. Later he attended the three liberal seminaries of Chicago, Oberlin, and Boston, and studied in depth the many aspects of liberalism.

Liberal theology had generated much dispute long before the Bukers entered Bates, and had made such an impact on evangelical Christianity in the early 1900s that a counterattack was launched by the conservatives in 1910. The doctrines on which they based their counterattack were basically six in number:

1. The authority of Scripture
2. The deity of Christ
3. The virgin birth of Jesus Christ
4. The substitutionary atonement of Jesus Christ
5. The resurrection of Jesus Christ
6. The second coming of our Lord in glory

The opening broadside of the counterattack was a series of twelve small books that were written by sixty-four conservative authors of wide and varied backgrounds. Among them were such men as the evangelist R. A. Torrey, Baptist theologians A. C. Dixon and E. Y. Mullins, and Presbyterians such as B. B. Warfield. These books were published between 1910 and 1915, and were financed by two wealthy brothers from California, named Stewart. Eventually the astonishing total of 3,000,000 copies was sent out free to theologians, theological students, ministers, and Christian workers.

These books were entitled "The Fundamentals," and were a thoughtful, thorough defense by theological giants of the six doctrines mentioned above. The books by no means ended the controversy but did provide a huge supply of ammunition for the conservatives. The battle increased in intensity through the 1920s and well into the 1940s. It affected a number of denominations, especially the Baptists and the Presbyterians. One of the central figures on the liberal side was a Baptist who was a visiting pastor of Riverside Baptist Church in New York City and a professor at Union Theological Seminary in New York, Harry Emerson Fosdick. The books "The Fundamentals" led to conservatives being called the Fundamentalists, and this was for the most part a term they gladly accepted at that time. Often the debate was conducted in a gentlemanly way; then again it was vitriolic, and intemperate language more suited to the gutter than the pulpit was used. It is significant to note that liberalism, which sprang from higher criticism, had its roots in Germany and later spread to Britain and America. The great Baptist preacher and pastor of the nineteenth century (some would say the greatest who ever lived) was Charles Haddon Spurgeon. He was a thorough Calvinist, a great student of the Puritans, and an outstanding pastor. For thirty-eight years, Sunday after Sunday, and in the same church, he preached to a congregation of 6,000 people. His sermons were printed in a number of languages, and it is estimated that through preaching and the printed sermons he reached one million people every week, and he did this for thirty-eight years, a feat never equalled before or since. Between 1887 and 1889 he was so concerned that theological liberalism was prevalent in the Baptist Union of Britain that he preached a series of sermons on what he called the "Downgrade in the Theology of the Baptist Union." His preaching began a fierce conflict, but did little to impede the trend toward liberalism. Therefore he and other Baptist pastors resigned from the Baptist Union in October of 1887, and the Union then passed a vote of censure on him which was never rescinded. He spent the remainder of his life as an independent Baptist. The "Downgrade Controversy" took its toll on his health, and many think that it shortened his life. It is ironic, and some would say hypocritical, that a bust of Spurgeon is prominent in the headquarters of the Baptist Union today. When his voice was silenced by death, they became eager to claim him as one of their sons. There is little doubt that had he been able to express his views, that bust would not be where it is.

In 1888 Spurgeon wrote, "Every Union, unless it is a mere fiction, must be based upon certain principles. How can we unite except upon some great common truths? And the doctrine of baptism by immersion is not sufficient for a groundwork. Surely, to be a Baptist is not everything. If I disagree with a man on ninety-nine points, but happen to be one with him in baptism, this can never furnish such ground of unity as I have with another with whom I believe in ninety-nine points, and only happen to differ upon one ordinance. . . . To alter the foundation of a building is a difficult undertaking. Underpinning is expensive and perilous work. It might be more satisfactory to take the whole house down, and reconstruct it. But *my* conscience is no guide for others. Those who believe in the structure, and think they can rectify its foundation, have my hearty sympathy in the attempt."

Later, in July 1889, he wrote even more decisively: "The day will come when those who think they can repair a house which has no foundations will see the wisdom of quitting it altogether. All along we have seen that to come out from association with questionable doctrines is the only possible solution of a difficulty which, however it may be denied, is not to be trifled with by those who are conscious of its terrible reality."

The battle started by Spurgeon in 1887 still continues to this day. *The Evangelical Times* of November 1979 carried the news that Lansdowne Baptist Church, of Bournemouth, England, had decided to leave the Baptist Union. This is a large and influential church on the south coast of England. "Those who will not learn from the past," wrote the philosopher George Santayana, "are condemned to re-live it." Tragically, it seems that even in our day, many so-called evangelicals have still failed to learn from the history of the last century, and even from the events of the 1930s and 1940s. Surely all the greater is their responsibility for which they must answer to our God. The price of retaining true evangelical purity is still constant vigilance.

What Spurgeon had pleaded for was a denomination that was built on a solid theological foundation, but historically the Baptists had not been a denomination based on a doctrinal statement. What had taken place in England was exactly what happened later to the American Baptists when strong conservative evangelicals discovered that the only common ground they shared with many of their colleagues was that of believer's baptism by immersion. To leave the denomination meant not only a great emotional trauma but also the sacrifice of pension rights. Ray was thoroughly aware of all these facts. As far back as his time at Bates he was ridiculed by some as being old-fashioned, primarily because he had never allowed himself to be exposed to more advanced thinking. There had also been the grim year at Chicago where he had seen the ugliest side of liberalism.

Why then did Ray embark on a career in a denomination that he knew to be so riddled with liberalism? He says that he was thoroughly informed about the whole situation, and that he had made his decision after a great deal of thought and prayer. Although liberalism was flourishing within the ranks of the American Baptists, there were hundreds of pastors and churches that were convinced, conservative evangelicals. In New England, for example, liberalism was having an initial influence on the churches, especially on the educational institutions.

There were hundreds of pastors who wanted more conservative missionaries to represent them on the field and they were delighted when the Buker twins volunteered. The Bukers had a very strong and wide base of support and it was in these churches that they spoke before they went to Burma.

Moreover, Ray had demonstrated that he could acquit himself well when he was attacked by liberals during his three years of seminary training. Another factor was that he knew there were liberal missionaries in Burma but that he would be working hundreds of miles from them.

Only three months after his arrival in Burma he had already quietly assessed the theological climate of the missionaries and various institutions in Rangoon and southern Burma. This assessment he expressed clearly in a private letter to his father and concluded that the vast majority were theologically liberal. In northern Burma he himself was surrounded by conservative missionaries and felt that in the jungle he could keep his distance from liberalism. He could not possibly foresee the future and imagine the great response there would be to his ministry. Later he found himself in a dilemma as to where he could send potential national leaders for further training that would be free from the influence of liberalism. Such problems he could not anticipate as the Bukers left Boston to begin a new chapter of their lives.

It would be misleading to give the impression that the controversy between liberals and conservatives was limited to the Baptists. On the contrary, it caused a great crisis among the Presbyterians that led to a revolt, which in turn forced a break much earlier than that of the Baptists.

The center of the storm was Princeton Seminary, which had produced a large number of distinguished theologians of the Reformed school of thought, such as Charles Hodge and B. B. Warfield. The trend toward liberal theology caused great controversy and led to the resignation of Gresham Machen, who had taught at Princeton since 1906. His resignation in 1929 led to the formation of Westminster Seminary in Philadelphia with an outstanding faculty that included Drs. Wilson, Allis, Stonehouse, Van Til, R. B. Kuiper, Woolley, and Murray. Machen himself served as president and professor of New Testament, and during this time some Princeton students transferred to Westminster.

In 1935 Machen was tried and found guilty of insubordination by a presbytery at Trenton, New Jersey, and by the General Assembly of the Presbyterian Church in the USA. He was not permitted to defend himself and was suspended from the PCUSA ministry. The action was strangely reminiscent of the treatment of Charles Spurgeon in England in the previous century. Machen later became a principal founder of the Orthodox Presbyterian Church in 1936.

Toward the end of the 1920s, the theological controversy among the Baptists in the United States raged with increasing fierceness. To a large extent this battle was fought mainly by pastors and churches, but there was one significant exception. A decision was made by the American Baptist Foreign Mission Society to send a leading fundamentalist pastor on a tour of all their mission fields to determine if liberal theology had affected the missionaries. The man chosen was Dr. Earle Pierce, the pastor of a Minneapolis church, a member of the board of the mission society, and the president of the National Fundamentalist Society. A few of the fields were thoroughly sound, some completely liberal, and others, like Burma, mixed.

The liberal element took pains to hide their true theological position. Certain people in each field whom the liberals considered safe and discreet were advised that when Dr. Pierce arrived in their area they should be careful to use fundamentalist language and talk about the blood of Jesus Christ and His atonement.

Most Christians will be shocked to learn that such unscrupulous tactics were used by missionaries, and rightly so. Some will doubtless question whether this subterfuge could possibly succeed, but it did, and Dr. Pierce was completely deceived. Those who have visited numerous mission fields and have been called on to evaluate some of them know that such a scheme is relatively simple. Most visitors to mission fields correctly start out with the basic conviction that, though human, the missionary is a person who has made a real sacrifice for the sake of Jesus Christ to serve overseas. The visitor is a guest of the missionary and sees people and events through the eyes of the missionary. The visitor does not know the local languages, so even when the visitor is sincere, his conclusions have been filtered through the views of the missionary.

Dr. Pierce had one other great difficulty. He was a member of the board of the American Baptist Foreign Mission Society and had interviewed the missionary candidates before they went overseas. Subconsciously it was probably difficult for him to admit that the people he was partly responsible for accepting for missionary service were not truly sound in their theology.

In Burma he visited only Rangoon, while Ray Buker, the conservative theologian, was buried in the jungle nearly 1,000 tough miles away. In South Burma there was a young missionary named Joe Smith, who had been a member of Dr. Pierce's home church. When Ray met this 6'4" conservative missionary some months later, Ray asked him if he had given a full description of the situation to Dr. Pierce. The missionary explained, "Ray, by the time I got to speak to him he had been thoroughly brainwashed, and his mind was made up. He merely regarded me as an inexperienced novice who was trying to rock the boat."

When Dr. Pierce arrived home in America, he announced that the missionary work in every field was thoroughly sound theologically, including China, where it was widely known that the work was directed by theologically liberal missionaries. He was a leading fundamentalist pastor, and other pastors accepted his verdict with uncritical relief. The deliberate cover-up carefully planned by the liberal officials had worked perfectly. What the result would have been if Dr. Pierce had met Ray, who had been immersed in the atmosphere of liberal seminaries and had survived, we shall never know. It was probably a pity that Dr. Pierce was not accompanied by another fundamentalist who might have been able to provide different insights.

# 5

## TRANSITION

Ray had first received a call to missionary work through a missionary to South America and he had kept that continent as his goal through college and seminary

While in prep school at Mount Hermon, Dick had received a call to missionary service prior to Ray's experience. They had both been exposed to some of the greatest missionary speakers of that period—men such as John Mott, Robert Wilder, and Robert Speer. To Dick, being a missionary was synonymous with teaching and preaching, but whenever he attempted to speak, or even pray in public, words failed him. He would put a few words together in his mind, repeat them, and eventually come to a humiliating close. To aggravate the situation, Ray was busy as a member of small groups of students who took services in local preaching points while he was at Mount Hermon. The problem seemed insoluble as well as humiliating to Dick; he had been called to be a missionary but could not speak in public. It was a paradox he could not solve.

Then Dick attended a Student Volunteer Convention and heard the great apostle to the Muslims, Dr. Samuel Zwemer, speak about the enormous potential of medical missionary work. In a moment Dick's problem was solved. He decided to become a doctor. As a medical missionary he would not have to preach. As we have seen, he was accepted at Harvard Medical School and eventually completed his studies for the M.D. degree. Later, he found however that in addition to becoming a medical missionary, he could also preach. God led him through a strange path to his vocation.

Early in 1925, when Ray was approaching the end of his seminary years, he weighed all the pros and cons of different fields of service and also various mission boards. The American Baptist Foreign Mission Society had no work in South America. Ray was a baptist through and through and never seriously considered serving with a "faith mission." He was prepared to serve with the Canadian Baptists, who had work in Bolivia. He decided that he would at least explain to his denominational mission board. So he wrote to the Foreign Secretary of the American Baptists, Dr. Joseph C. Robbins. Dr. Robbins' account of his first encounter with the Buker twins is contained in the following brief article.

### The Story of the Buker Twins
by Foreign Secretary Joseph C. Robbins

Early in 1925, I received a letter from Rev. Raymond Buker, in which he said: "You probably don't remember me, but I was one of your aides at the Student Volunteer Convention in Indianapolis. It may help you to remember me if I remind you that I am the champion mile runner of America. I am to run one more race in San Francisco, the 4th of July, 1925, and then I wish to go to the most difficult mission field in the world. I wish to talk to you about it, and I must have more than twenty minutes of your time."

Fortunately, I was to go to Boston within a few days, and so it was possible for me to arrange to meet this young man there. When he came to my room at the hotel, I said to him, "How did you happen to become a runner?" He then replied, "I found I could run when I was in college, and I became the champion of Bates College, then the champion of the State of Maine, then champion of New England, then champion of America, which admitted me to the Olympic Team, and I won fifth place in the Olympics." Then he said, "Would you like to see me run?" Of course, I said that I should, and together we went to a nearby track and I watched him as he ran the half mile in 2 minutes, 7 seconds.

We returned to the hotel, and he said, "Now where will I go as a missionary?" I told him of a far distant field on the border of Burma and remote West China, among the Lahu and Wa people, sturdy mountain tribes, where there has been a great ingathering—17,500 having been baptized and received into the church there in the last five years. I told him of the persecution and hardships of that field, and he said, "Mr. Robbins, do you think I am the man for that difficult work?" I said, "Let us pray together about it." We knelt together in that hotel room and prayed, and when we arose from our knees, he said, "Do you need a physician in the same field?" I said, "We certainly should have a doctor there." "My twin brother is a doctor: will you take him?" he asked. I replied that I should have to see him first, and he said that they looked so much alike that I should be unable to tell them apart.

Then he invited me to come over to his home to meet his wife, his brother and his wife, and also his father and mother. I found it possible to do so, and so I made the arrangement to meet Dr. and Mrs. Richard Buker, Rev. and Mrs. Raymond Buker, and father and mother Buker in their home.

I told them frankly and plainly of the isolation, hardship and danger of this field, back as it is twenty-three days from civilization in the heart of the mountains of West China. Mrs. Richard Buker looked up and said, "Mr. Robbins, you have not painted a very bright picture." I said, "No. All I can promise you is isolation, loneliness, hardship, sacrifice, suffering;" and then, I am ashamed to say, I had to add (for I try to be honest and frank with all our missionary candidates), "I cannot promise that the denomination will support you adequately." And then these four young people said to me, "We will go."

In May 1925, the twins and their wives were accepted for service on the border between Burma and China. Since Dorothy was pregnant, the mission advised Ray to wait until the baby came. Accordingly he took a pastorate in New England for nine months, and then proceeded to Burma.

In September of that year, Ray accepted the pastorate of three Baptist churches in Maine: Sabattus, Wales, and South Monmouth. The Sabattus church with only twenty-one members was about to close its doors. This was to be a last-ditch effort to maintain the church. They bought a parsonage for Ray and Dorothy and rallied to continue services. Ray's grandfather had been a deacon of the Sabattus church. Each of the three churches was almost fiercely independent, so Ray had to receive a separate call to each of the three churches.

He began his ministry with a strong emphasis on pastoral visitation. He simply went to every house in the community and greeted whoever happened to be home. One man exclaimed that he had lived in his home for thirty years and had never had a pastor visit him. Fifty years later people still talk about this aspect of Ray's ministry. His experience in visitation was very rewarding and people reacted positively. However, not everyone accepted the invitation to go to church. The results in Wales and South Monmouth were not as encouraging as in Sabattus, but in that village there was a heartwarming response. The membership increased to triple its original size. For both church and pastor it was a wonderful experience, and soon the small church was filled, often one hundred in the morning and sixty or so in the evening. For the evening service Ray cleared everything from the platform and just preached his heart out. It was the first time he had had such an opportunity and he rose to it. The people responded and some of them came forward weeping when the invitation was given. Ray, knowing that the usual New Englander is reserved and cautious, revelled in the whole experience and marveled in the fact that God was using him in this way. He was ever thankful to God for this pastorate. Later on, his studies in two other languages, he believed, blunted the edge of his preaching ability in English.

The ministry in these country churches was a special time in the life of Ray and Dorothy. God worked through Ray's preaching in an exceptional way, for he had never experienced such evangelistic fruitfulness among his many athletic friends, and he never had such a time again. In later life as a missionary he baptized hundreds of converts, but he insists that his gifts at that time were as a helper and administrator who trained and organized others to carry out the actual evangelism. His honesty about his gifts was to get him into hot water thirty years later, as we shall see.

Ray and Dorothy's only child, Raymond Bates Buker, Junior, was born on December 26, 1925, during their pastorate in Maine. Those months were happy months for them. The congregations responded to them and loved them, so much so, they felt strongly that Ray had no right to go to a mission field in Burma when God was using him so powerfully in the mission field in Maine. One Scottish deacon was particularly aggressive, insisting, "You have no right to leave this place where God is using you and go elsewhere to work. I have as much right to know the will of God as you do."

To be so used and to feel so loved must surely have tempted Ray to stay and continue the work he was enjoying, but though it was at least nine years since he had received the call to the mission field, there was never any deviation from that inescapable revelation from God. Like many missionaries, he was to go through times of self-doubt, but then he would always be able to look back to this period in his life and feel that God had proved that he had spiritual gifts. Ray had learned many valuable lessons from his pastorate, and in later years he would suggest to many missionary recruits that they first obtain experience in Christian service in the United States before leaving for their field. This advice was heeded by Ray Junior who accepted a pastorate before going to Pakistan as a missionary.

On September 18, 1926, the Buker families finally left for Burma and their first term of service, boarding the SS *Franconia*, of the famous Cunard Line, in Boston. From Boston they sailed to Liverpool, England, with a brief stop in Halifax, Nova Scotia. It was a trip they would long remember, because while crossing the Atlantic they were buffeted by the tail end of a hurricane which earlier had created great damage in Florida.

In Liverpool, at the end of September the weather was bleak, cold, and depressing. Heating facilities were curtailed, and the only way they could get any warmth was to run the hot water in the bath. They were fortunate to have this comfort. The year 1926 was the worst period for industrial unrest in Britain. The great economic depression was at its worst. The coal miners had been on strike for many months because their already meager pay was cut, and at this time the first and last general strike in British history was going on. Although the strike did not last long, it did paralyze transportation and cut off food and coal production. It also forced all newspapers to shut down, so the life of the entire nation was disrupted.

During their crowded four days in Liverpool they managed to spend one day visiting the town of Chester, a little to the south. In Britain every city that has a name ending with "chester," such as Winchester, Chichester, Colchester, was founded by the ancient Romans. It was in character that the Bukers took the opportunity to visit Chester, a beautiful and historical center dating back to Roman times.

On October 1 they sailed from Liverpool on the SS *Chindwin*, of the Henderson line, which ran a regular service to Egypt and Burma. Some of the letters Ray wrote home contained good descriptions of life on board ship. He gave a thorough account of all the deck sports that were available and the Bukers took advantage of them, even though most of these sports were new to them. Here they were introduced to British formality that required dress suits for dinner. Appropriate suits had been bought in Liverpool to meet this situation.

The *Chindwin* docked at Gibraltar where the new missionaries were introduced to Mediterranean life by the local vendors who rowed out to the ship to sell their wares. Soon they were on their way again. Their next stop was in the port of Oran, in Algeria, not far from Sidi-bel-Abbes, the headquarters of the famous French Foreign Legion. Here they had time to go ashore while the liner renewed its supply of coal for the furnaces. From here they were able to see the Atlas mountains of Africa and had their first glimpse of the Arab world.

Within a few days, as they passed the island of Malta just south of Sicily, Ray wrote home, "On Sunday we had a unique experience; we passed quite close to Malta. Out with all the binoculars we could muster, for we passed within sight of St. Paul's Bay. On the edge of the Bay was a monument visible through the glasses, with a cross upon it to mark the spot of Paul's landing after the shipwreck. Valletta is the capital containing one of the finest double harbors in the world. This is British territory.

"Just to think that this moment I am sailing over the sea, and maybe the very spot where Hannibal with his armies came to threaten Rome. Where the Caesars carried on their conquests, where Rome was dependent as a route for its grain, and most thrilling of all where Jonah and Paul may have sailed. Would that some mirage might restore a vision of the actuality. Soon we will cross the actual route of the Children of Israel as led by Jehovah, and Moses, the human leader, as they searched for the promised land.

"Oh, that I knew more and better of these things through which we are now passing and that they might be able to inspire me to the proper reaction."

From this letter we get a glimpse of Ray's intense curiosity and also see how he delighted to link his classical education with his current experiences.

In a later letter of October 27, dateline one week from Rangoon, he described some of his fellow passengers who totalled eighty in number, of which twenty-nine were missionaries. Giving a breakdown of the total number, Ray noted twenty-one were from the American Baptist Foreign Mission Society, six from the Society for the Propagation of the Gospel (SPG), a Church of England Missionary Society, and two from the Bible Churchman's Missionary Society (BCMS).

Ray gave further details of fellow American Baptist missionaries, describing one individual, whom we shall meet later, as follows: "Next we come to Rev. Joseph M. Smith. Perhaps we are forced to because of his size. Six feet four inches in his stocking feet, he provides an able physical guard to our party. Joe brings with him a splendid family. . . . When Joe became the pastor of the church in Mound, Minnesota, they debated for some time what name to put outside the church. Joseph M. Smith* would tend to give an impression of Mormonism. Accordingly they decided upon Rev. J. M. Smith." Joe and Ray were to become warm friends with identical views on theology.

Ray wrote frankly to his father and family: "Our own older Baptist missionaries are much more influenced by modernism." Perhaps the most significant missionaries who drastically affected some of his future decisions were British, and members of the Church of England. Ray wrote to his father, "There are two missionaries from the Bible Churchman's Missionary Society (BCMS); this is the fun-

---

*A reference to Joseph Smith, founder of the Mormons.

damentalist group of the Church of England. The history during the last four years of this group is very interesting. They have had to break away and form their own organization because of the modernism coming so strongly into the theological seminaries of England. It is hard to get ordained men for the BCMS. But during the last few years the SPG have had to retrench for lack of men, money, and conditions on the field. But the BCMS have increased and now have forty-two men on the field and have money almost unlimited. These two young representatives on this boat, unmarried, are splendid chaps and I get a lot of spiritual help from them. Our own older missionaries are much influenced by modernism, though some are still evangelical and evangelistic, believing in the deity of Christ. Fowler and Rushton, the BCMS men, are going away up in the hills north of Mandalay."

The idea of one denomination having two or more missionary societies, at least one of which was theologically, conservative, was a revelation to Ray. Not only did he write of it to his father, but it was never far from his thoughts in years to come.

# 6

## FIRST TERM

In early November the Bukers finally reached the Bay of Bengal in which the Irrawaddy River of Burma flows, docking at Rangoon, the capital of Burma. It is a country approximately the size of New England or the British Isles, with an estimated population of seventeen million, and is surrounded by Siam (now Thailand) to the south, China to the north and east, and India to the north and west.

The historic rulers of the country were the Burmese, who were Buddhists, and who were very resistant to the gospel. The second largest group were the Karen tribe, despised by the Burmese. The Karens were also the first people to respond to the gospel. When Ray arrived in Burma they had a strong, indigenous church that sent missionaries to other tribes and races in the north of Burma. The Karens also had the complete Bible translated into their dialect. Ray was to work with the many tribes that existed to the northeast and especially in the mountains on the border of Burma and Yunnan. In fact, most of his first term of service was spent in Yunnan rather than in Burma, at the Meng Meng station. A census taken in 1921 revealed that Christians, both Roman Catholic and Protestant, constituted only 2 percent of the population.

Burma was a British possession and for administrative purposes the British linked it with their control of India, giving to the Burmese a limited degree of self-rule. A British parliamentary commission was sent to India and Burma in 1927 and 1928, which decided that the link between India and Burma was unwieldy and recommended that it be abolished. Their advice was rejected by the British cabinet, and in World War II the whole administrative machinery was partially responsible for the disastrous defeat suffered at the hands of the Japanese. The British governor of Burma was Sir Reginald Dorman-Smith, and during the war he wrote, "It is definitely disappointing that after all of our years of occupation . . . we have not been able to create that loyalty which is generally associated with our subject races." A British historian added, "His very choice of words, perhaps, explains why." Dorman-Smith's patronizing attitude was characteristic of many of the officials the Bukers had to deal with from time to time.

In 1806 William Carey encouraged his son Felix to enter Burma. Felix's stay in Burma was as a British government consul.

The first group of missionaries ever to leave America to sail overseas was a group of four, of whom one was the brilliant Adoniram Judson. He was sent out by the Congregational Church in 1812 and planned to work in India. Knowing that he would have dealings with William Carey who was a British Baptist, he devoted much time during the long voyage in studying the subject of believer's baptism by immersion so that he could more thoroughly understand Carey. The result of his study led him to conclude that the position of William Carey was correct. When he arrived in India he was immersed in Calcutta by William Ward, another British Baptist. This decision was to have far-reaching effects. He was later excluded from India by the hostility of the British East India Company and, after several attempts, he landed in Rangoon in July 1813, having obtained the support of the American Baptists.

Judson founded the work of the American Baptists in

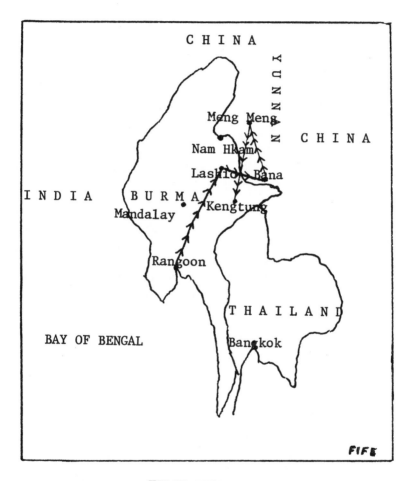

FIRST TERM

Burma and eventually, despite great personal suffering, translated the entire Bible into Burmese and compiled an English-Burmese dictionary. By the time the Buker family arrived, the American Baptists had two hundred missionaries in Burma, and were so well established that they had their own banking system. They organized rest homes, complete with British-trained butlers, finger bowls, and afternoon tea at 4 P.M. The ABM was so reliable that their checks were more acceptable than checks by British banks. The Bukers had to adjust not only to different native customs, but to the British customs as well.

Ray was eventually to work with a number of different tribes, including the Lahu, the Shan (Tai, whose languages Ray learned), and the Wa, Ahka, Tai Loi, Kachin, and of course with the Burmese, the Chinese, and the Karens. He became the only white man to learn Tai Khun, and translated the Gospels of John and Mark into that dialect. He also had contacts with the Lisu tribe in China, although he did not work with them.

Burma is a country consisting of range after range of towering mountains, many of them with altitudes of well over 10,000 feet. The mountains were covered by dense jungle and intersected by great rivers such as the Chindwin, the Irrawaddy, the Salween, and the Mekong. Travel in the country was difficult as there were only narrow trails, most of them not more than three feet wide. Journeys were calculated in hours or days rather than in miles because it involved climbing and descending a series of mountain ranges. When the traveler reached the top of one range, he saw only another steep descent, often as steep as the roof of a New England house, and then the heartbreaking prospect of another towering mountain range to be climbed. Ray had asked for a difficult field, and he certainly got it.

The Bukers arrived in Burma in November 1926. As the ship sailed the forty miles up the Irrawaddy River to the port of Rangoon, they gazed with more than usual curiosity at the country in which they were investing their lives. They could see on the right bank of the river the great Buddha of Shwe Dagon (pagoda) dominating everything, including Rangoon.

Once in Rangoon, it didn't take the Bukers long to become aware of some of the problems and novelties of living and working in a land with foreign customs and languages, and the problems were complicated by the fact that the new missionaries had young children. Enough English was spoken for them to make simple shopping trips and, of course, there were other missionaries there to assist them. They helped the Bukers with the purchasing of tents, tropical clothes, and supplies, for their destination was in Bana, in China, a thousand miles and a three-week journey from Rangoon. Preparations were completed about November 15, and the Bukers then left Rangoon on their long journey.

During the first term in the field Dick and Ray were rarely to work together, but they left on this journey as a party with Mr. Vincent Young and his brother and wife, Mr. and Mrs. Harold Young. Their route took them to Mandalay, and from there to Lashio. It was here they ran into their first great obstacle. Many rains had caused them to leave the train to Mandalay and travel by river boat up the Irrawaddy. The beauty of the pagoda-lined riverbanks amply repaid the inconvenience.

From Mandalay they proceeded to the lovely hill station of Maymyo. While they waited, William Young arrived in Lashio from Bana to buy ponies and travel supplies, but it wasn't long after they set out on the ponies that they discovered traveling was a nightmare. The children were a special problem. The usual way to travel in Burma and most other Third World countries was to carry the children strapped to the back. However, the Bukers did not want their children strapped all day to the sweaty back of one of the carriers, so they decided to use a dooly. This was a large crib with long legs, fitted with long poles on the sides so that two men could carry each child.

Each morning the beds and tents had to be taken down and made into pony packs. The men were weighed down with guns and various bags and boxes, and each evening everything had to be unloaded again.

The Bukers had much to learn about jungle traveling, but that would come only with experience. In the words of Dick, they had not learned to travel light.

While at Lashio Ray was apparently bitten by a mosquito, which could have proved fatal to him. Mosquitoes were plentiful in that humid climate, and the usual form of malaria that resulted was tertiary, which means that the victim could be very ill for one day with chills and a high temperature, and then be quite well the next two days. So he would be ill every third day. There is another form of malaria in which the victim is ill one day and well the next day, but in which with most types of malaria the temperature and chills would appear about noon. Ray became ill, but Dick had difficulty in diagnosing it as the symptoms did not fit any type he had studied. Sometimes the chills and temperatures would come at night and he would be better during the day; at other times he would have intermittent chills and temperatures several days in a row. Dick had studied malaria at Harvard Medical School but had never treated a case before, and without being able to diagnose Ray's illness, he naturally found it difficult to treat. Of course, on a journey like theirs it was impossible to find a microscope and do blood examinations. In fact, in frontier medical work this was always a serious difficulty, and the diagnosis usually had to be made on the basis of clinical observation. Dick began to realize that his twin brother was very ill, so in desperation he started giving him quinine, ten grains three times a day. By the second day Ray was much better.

It was proved later that he was suffering from malignant malaria, and it was a real ordeal to travel under such a handicap. Malaria was so rampant in Burma that later Dick formed the practice of giving all his patients malaria treatment whatever their complaint, because they were certain to suffer from malaria sooner or later. He also discovered that, good though his medical education had been, there was much that could be learned only by experience.

Two illustrations from World War II vividly demonstrate how common and deadly malaria was in many parts of the world and also the price it can extract. In 1943 the American and British armies invaded Sicily in the Mediterranean, and in two months they had lost the equivalent of two infantry divisions because they contracted malaria and had to be evacuated. In New Guinea, 47,534 men had to be evacuated and of that number only 3,140 were battle casualties; the rest had been stricken with malaria.

Eventually the doolies had to be given up as they were not practical and the children were strapped to the backs of carriers after all. On December 19 the party crossed the border from Burma into Yunnan, China, and on December 22 they rode into the mission compound at Bana.

To the Bukers' consternation they discovered that there was only one missionary home for three married couples, two babies, and two single men. The two Buker families had to share one large room with a curtain down the middle. Writing to his hometown paper, the Pawtuxet Valley *Daily Times*, the next day, Ray gave a vivid account of their experiences. In describing their exhausting journey over mountain tops that were above the clouds he compared it with the tinsel and lights of a typical American Christmas, and contrasted the beauty of the mountains with the bright lights of Main Street, USA. He concluded the article with, "Folks may think it was terrible for me to ride along very sick, but they would not think it bad for me to run a race and feel all exhausted. On those three days of traveling with malaria in my system, I felt exactly as I used to feel in the days of my races, before, during, and after the race. If I could suffer then for the sake of a sport, how much more ought I be willing to suffer for the work of my Lord?"

He also wrote to his father and expressed his impressions of some of the missionaries he had met on the voyage, during their month in Rangoon, and during the brief time he had spent in the Maymyo Rest House. He noted that in southern Burma there was much theological liberalism and that it was particularly true of the educational institutions. Because of his temperament he got along well with others, but with his keen powers of observation nothing had gone unnoticed. He went on to write that as his work was in the north, on the border of Burma and China, he could bury himself in the jungle and thus be far away from the liberalism that characterized his colleagues in lower Burma.

This revealed his keen awareness of the serious theological problems present among the Burma missionaries, but he didn't then realize that among many of the people with whom he would work some would sooner or later need training in Bible and theology and thus would be exposed to this theological laxity. However, all in all, it showed that this recruit to the missionary force of the Burmese field of the American Baptist Mission had above average powers of observation. All too often a recruit is so aware of the large areas of his limited knowledge and is so obsessed with the novelty of a new country that he takes all things at their face value.

Ray always demonstrated two qualities that are rarely found in one person: penetrating insight coupled with a gentle and modest spirit that avoided conflict whenever possible.

After having been in Bana about a month, Ray accompanied the veteran missionary, William Young, father of Vincent and Harold, on a tour through the area. Mr. Young had been mightily used of God in the mass movement to Christ of the Lahu tribe. There had been 40,000 baptisms, and in 1926 alone 5,000 were baptized under his ministry. He was a rugged man with experience that was matched only by his zeal for the work. He was a widower, and his two sons, now fully grown, had become missionaries themselves. Because there was not much family life for him he was quite willing to be away from his home base for long periods of time.

So he and Ray left for Ray's first tour. When they would arrive at a village, William would preach, and after the meeting would sit "in court" while the Lahu villagers brought to him their problems and troubles. The next morning he would go down to the river and baptize any candidates who were ready. If there were none, the two men would set out early for the day's journey to the next village. To Ray it was a great revelation and he learned much from observing the veteran at work. He later learned from his own experiences, however, that there was much about the work of Mr. Young that was dictatorial and therefore had serious limitations, but for the time being Ray continued to observe and learn.

As the tour continued longer and longer Ray began to feel uncomfortable. It had been planned as a two-month trip, but at that time his senior showed no intention of returning. Ray often worried about Dorothy and his one-year-old son back in Bana. He wondered how they were adjusting to their new conditions and how their health was.

Ray eventually mentioned his misgivings to Mr. Young, but he fully intended to press on. Eventually, Ray felt so strongly about the matter that he decided to leave Mr. Young and take his own ponies and carriers and head for Bana. The decision was not an easy one. They were in the Yunnan province of China, with many bandits about, and Ray knew little of the language. The decision was not popular with Mr. Young.

They went their separate ways. Ray had been on the return journey only a day or two when he received news that there was serious trouble in Bana where he had left his family. The Chinese bandits were threatening to destroy the mission station because they were angry with the missionaries. Dorothy was in danger after only three months on the field. Within three or four hours he was overtaken by Mr. Young who had also heard the news and had changed all his plans and was returning as fast as he could. Once more they were together and made forced marches that consisted of traveling the equivalent of two days in one. It meant rising at 4 A.M. and traveling until sunset. As a result, they arrived home fairly soon, but the ponies died of exhaustion. The two missionaries arrived at the same time. Ray had not shaved for a month or so, and looked disheveled. Mr. Young was leading the caravan as usual when they approached the Bana compound, and then Ray saw Dorothy coming to meet them. Filled with joy and relief, he spurred his pony past Mr. Young to greet her. How wonderful it was to be reunited at last, and to learn that the danger had passed.

Dick was still at Bana and the Lahu clamored for his services, but he soon discovered that his medical work was very unpopular with some of the missionaries. One of them in particular did all he could to undermine Dick's work by delaying his orders for drugs. Dick still knew only a few phrases of the Lahu language that were needed to practice his medical work, and it was only later that he and Ray discovered to what extremes his critic would go. Once while Dick was examining a desperately ill baby, it died in his arms. The missionary complained in Lahu, "See, this white man has come to kill your children." This behavior seems incredible, and we can only assume that jealousy for his work had driven this fellow worker to such limits of unreasonableness. Dick consequently led a very difficult life at Bana. Indeed, both he and Ray were introduced to missionary work through a baptism of fire.

After working in Bana for more than a year, Dick was asked to move south to Kengtung across the border in Burma. The missionaries there were delighted to have him as they had a hospital, but needed a doctor badly. This meant that the Buker twins would now be separated by three hundred miles, and it would remain that way until the last year of their six-year term.

In the spring of 1927, Ray and Dorothy with Ray, Jr. left Bana to open the new station at Meng Meng, which was an eight-day journey from Bana. A bamboo house was their home while a permanent structure was being built. Although Ray knew nothing about building, he did have the assistance of one of the Young brothers during the first six months at Meng Meng. Meanwhile Ray was also learning the language.

Every day a large number of sick people would come for help, and Ray would hold a clinic for them. The tribespeople in these primitive areas did not know which missionary was a doctor, so to them every white man had some medicine and could help. Dick likens this to the way that doctors were trained on the frontiers of the West in the USA while it was being developed. If a person wanted to be a doctor, he would attach himself to a practicing doctor for a few years as an assistant. He would help with everything from taking care of the doctor's horse and stable to helping with the actual medical work. After some time he would strike out on his own as a doctor. According to Dick this was rough and ready medicine, but it was surprisingly successful in many cases. He knew of missionaries who had been so overwhelmed when besieged by sick people that they would use cough drops or even toothpaste because they had nothing else to give.

Ray was in a position to help because Dick had supplied him with medicines and much good advice. When he was faced with a difficult case, he would write long letters to Dick giving descriptions of the symptoms and also tell him what medicine he had given. The letter would take nearly two weeks to reach Dick, who would then write a detailed reply and suggest probable diagnosis and treatment. After a few months Ray became so proficient that Dick said he achieved a cure rate of 80 to 90 percent of the patients he treated.

The new field for Ray and Dorothy living at Meng Meng included 10,000 Lahu Christians in the San Kaishin area, east of Meng Meng, and 10,000 Wa Christians in Yunnan adjacent to the head-hunting Wa area, southwest of Meng Meng, which was centrally located in a Tai valley in Yunnan two days east of the Burma border.

Ray worked in Meng Meng for about three-and-one-half years. A year or so after arriving there, Dick visited him and Dorothy, and inspected the mission station. Dick was surprised to learn that Ray had mastered the Lahu language so well that when he would preach in English Ray interpreted into Lahu, reflecting an unusual ability in linguistics. It is interesting to imagine the effect on the tribespeople to see two white men who were identical in appearance, one speaking in English, the other in their native tongue. The people never were able to distinguish who was the doctor and who was the teacher.

During this time Ray was passing through a very difficult testing. Through the ministry of William Young and his two sons, thousands had accepted the Christian way of life and were scattered through the mountains in hundreds of villages. Many of these villages had churches and pastors whose salaries had for years been paid out of mission funds. Ray's task was to oversee all this work and to pay the salaries of the pastors. At this time the Depression was sweeping America and the money the mission was able to forward to the field was drastically reduced. Thus it became Ray's unpleasant duty to tell the pastors that their salaries had to be reduced. It is not surprising that they became disgruntled or even that some would conclude that Ray was receiving the money as usual, but that he was putting it in his own pocket. It took a long time before many were reassured that Ray was honest and was working solely for their own spiritual good. Even so, it was his heartbreaking experience to see countless villages and their pastors lapse back to their old heathen practices when their pastors left them. This was an age-old missionary problem that Ray had never been informed about in his training. Missionaries were finding that unscrupulous people frequently would profess conversion more for greed of money than out of spiritual conviction. A name had been coined for such people; they were called rice-Christians. They were "Christian" because of the rice given them by the missionaries.

Good would eventually come out of this experience, however, because Ray learned the hard way the difference between right and wrong missionary methods. During this time he continued his various activities, which included the clinic, language study, and an incredible amount of bookkeeping, translation work, and handling of correspondence. He also had the oversight of fifty Lahu and Wa pastors. To help them Ray wrote a catechism in Lahu for the instruction of young Christians, and prepared a monthly bulletin in their language. Weekends he would tour among the 10,000 Christian Lahu in nearby mountains. Dorothy would go along with him and, using a concertina, she would teach thousands of Christians to sing hymns. She also worked among the women and children. If you would have met this white-haired lady with dancing eyes and gentle manner years later, you would have found it difficult to picture her in rugged missionary work.

Two mountain ranges away in China, the China Inland Mission (now OMF) had their marvelous work among the Lisu. The work was superintended by an Englishman, James O. Frazer, who had pioneered the Lisu work in 1910, when he was twenty-four years old. The CIM workers were well aware of the great mass movement that the American Baptist missionaries had experienced among the Lahu and Wa, and they would occasionally cross the mountains to see these missionaries. Frazer himself had occasionally visited Burma, once for safety during a revolution, other times to obtain supplies, sometimes in connection with preparation for printing. As we have seen, Rangoon was only half as far as his headquarters in Shanghai.

On one occasion Carl Gowman and a colleague named Allyn Cooke paid a visit to Ray and Dorothy at Meng Meng, and Ray felt a close spiritual oneness with these godly people. The two men explained to Ray how unsatisfactory his missionary methods were compared to their own policies among the Lisu. Ray had simply continued with the methods as he had seen them exemplified by his Baptist seniors, but he was always open to new ideas. The fact that many pastors had gone back to idolatry made him even more receptive to advice.

When Ray and Dorothy had been at Meng Meng for about two years, Frazer came to visit them. He came to them walking, with only two Lisu carriers, who were usually unpaid volunteers. This surprised Ray because when he traveled, he took with him ten ponies, ten carriers, and his own riding ponies. His wife and son often went with him but he traveled like a king compared to the CIM missionaries.

Frazer had not been in the Buker home long when he noticed a small portable organ that had recently arrived from the States. He had great musical talents which had been buried in his jungle life. So when he had access to this little organ he sat down and played for an hour without a note of music in front of him. Ray and Dorothy knew of his musical gifts, but even so, they were astonished at the beautiful music he was able to produce. Ray, in referring to the incident, said, "It was like heaven on earth." It reminded them of the happy evenings they had experienced in the Oberlin Conservatory in 1923–1924.

Frazer and Ray had many discussions and one of them centered around the subject of guns. On the advise of senior American missionaries, Ray had obtained a .38 revolver, a rifle, a shotgun, and a high-powered .22 rifle that had such a high velocity that Ray once shot a deer in the neck from a distance of a quarter of a mile. He had a virtual arsenal of weapons, but began to have reservations about firearms, and thought to himself, "Is God trying to teach me something?" On one occasion on tour he had shot at bandits who had returned his fire with too much accuracy for comfort. When he raised the matter with Frazer, he learned that Frazer never carried a gun. He declared simply that he relied on God for his protection and explained the philosophy that lay behind this practice.

"If I carried a gun," said Frazer, "bandits would feel perfectly justified in shooting me, taking my gun, my life, and anything I possessed. When bandits appear, I tell them that I have come to bring good to their people, that I am a God-man, and if they shoot me, I am ready to die, but God will be displeased with them. I tell them that I am no trader, so I have little money and nothing valuable. They have always left me alone."

This may have sounded naive if it had been a raw recruit talking, but CIM tribal missionaries had followed this policy while working and traveling the past twenty years in a country infested with bandits. It not only showed keen insight, but was also a reflection of the utter dependence on God, qualities that built confidence in the work of the CIM.

Ray took Frazer outside where they looked at the mountains that surrounded them, and he shared with him his pent-up discouragement. He pointed to many villages that had once been Christian, but had now lapsed back to their old heathen practices. Ray spoke of his feeling of failure and was even considering resigning from the mission and returning to America because he could not pay the tribal pastors. This was entirely out of character for Ray because whenever he had met problems before, whether in track or in seminary, such as Chicago Divinity School, he had doggedly persevered until he had achieved his goal. Frazer could not have known that, but what he did see was a young missionary in distress.

It is interesting to speculate that Frazer could have taught Ray about missionary methods. He could have pointed out the fact that because of the policies that had been developed in the CIM work, the situation Ray was now facing could never have happened among the Lisu because they had never received missionary money in the first place. But that was not his way. When Ray finished his tale of woe, Frazer was silent. He made no comment on the situation.

When he and Dorothy went to bed that night, Ray poured out his disappointment to her. "I told him all about our problems, and he said nothing. He doesn't know the answer any more than I do."

The next day Frazer and Ray went for a walk, and then Frazer said to him, "Yesterday you told me about your problems. I would like to ask you a question. Whose work is this: yours or God's?"

Without hesitation, Ray replied, "It is God's."

Frazer answered, "He who hath begun a good work in you will perform it until the day of Jesus Christ." Ray reports that at that moment a great burden rolled off him and never returned. Years later Ray said of this incident, "Frazer was a man sent from God, and the one verse he quoted, Philippians 1:6, was like a shaft of light." To Frazer, methods were extremely important, but spiritual issues came first. Years later, as Ray was recounting this incident, he was asked if he had come to understand the reason for Frazer's silence at first. Ray replied without hesitation.

"Of course. Frazer was a man who never spoke about a problem without a period of prayer and thought. Second, he was a guest of the American Baptists and I never heard him utter a word of criticism of them or their policies, even though I knew that in South Burma there were many policies and theological views that must have been distasteful for him. To me he exercised a pastoral ministry. It was the Americans who worked under Frazer's leadership who could tell me kindly, but bluntly, where my methods were wrong."

Frazer's attitude of courteous reticence toward the methods of the American Baptists raises the question if Ray would have ever learned the advanced missionary methods if

Frazer had not had American colleagues. The question is academic, but interesting. There seem to be two parts to the answer, one theological, the other pragmatic.

First, Ray is a Calvinist, and therefore he believes nothing happens by chance. Therefore it was easy for him to see that God in His sovereign will would have overruled and met the need, whatever method or people He chose to use.

Second, Ray was convinced that the methods the American Baptists used were self-defeating, and so he was constantly looking for ways to improve. The Buker twins were creative; Dick showed he was very willing and determined to pioneer innovative methods for medical work among the leprosy patients, and Ray was as creative as his brother. One of the subjects he chose to study in depth during his first furlough was cultural anthropology. He says he cannot remember a time in his life when he was not a voracious and disciplined reader. Even during the busiest times of his life, he had a settled policy of reading something during every day, apart from his regular reading of the Scripture. In recent years he has planned on fifty pages every day. This combination of facts makes it certain that he would have pioneered innovative methods personally as Frazer had done, and as Dick was doing in the fields of leprosy treatment.

Ray began to make journeys across the two ranges of mountains that separated him from the Lisu work of the CIM. He valued greatly the wonderful fellowship he had with the CIM missionaries but he also found some answers to his questions. Ray saw the contrast between their approach and the one that he was using among the Lahu, and he realized that if similar methods had been applied among his own people his problems would have been greatly modified.

Frazer seems to have developed his own methods. Roland Allen's first book on missionary methods was not published until 1912 and Frazer could not have received a copy before the end of World War I in 1918. Perhaps he had read about Nevius and his indigenous methods in the previous century. By the time he could have obtained a copy of Allen's book, his methods among the Lisu were well developed. His letters and biography reveal his creativity in many ways. He observed the orthodox missionary methods, and if they were not successful he was willing to scrap them, trying a different approach. Over the years the different ways proved to be good for the Lisu work.

It is not surprising that Ray, during his study of missions in seminary, had not been exposed to indigenous methods somewhere. It seems inexcusable that many missionary agencies continued to operate with the tired, old methods until the 1960s. And in some cases they still adhere to them.

Ray had received one of the best educations a man could get, but though the Cookes and the Gowmans had been able to attend only Bible institutes, they soon learned much more about missionary methods by simply following the example that Frazer set. When Ray was eventually placed in the position to teach younger missionaries, it is not surprising that the biography of J. O. Frazer, *Behind the Ranges*, became required reading for all appointees.

Ray put to good use in his second tour of service the missionary methods he learned in his first term and these lessons eventually formed the basis of his teaching to scores of young missionaries who went to the field under his influence years later.

By this time Ray rarely rode when he traveled. He found that he could walk faster than the ponies and usually walked in front with Dorothy riding a pony, then the pack animals following them.

J. O. Frazer and the Allyn Cookes were blessed by the Lord with many spiritual gifts and were glad to "bury" these gifts in the jungle so that thousands of Lisu and Lahu would not only accept the gospel but would become teachers, evangelists, and missionaries to other Lisu groups, all supported by their own people.

The Lisu were a gifted musical race by nature and under the influence of Frazer and Cooke became such wonderful singing groups that people report they learned not only hymns but also the *Messiah.* To hear them singing the "Hallelujah Chorus" was a sublime experience. Later, some of the work of the American Baptists among the Lahu was transferred to the CIM with Allyn Cooke in charge.

Ray had learned much about missionary methods from the Cookes and other CIM workers and also from his thorough and careful study of Roland Allen's book *Missionary Methods: St. Paul's or Ours?* which he had ordered from America. For the rest of his life Ray acknowledged that much that he knew about missionary methods he learned from the CIM, and as we have seen this was largely true, especially at the beginning. However, this typically modest statement obscures a life-long research of anthropology, and above all his intense examination of missionary methods on the field. This began with a study of his own work but later through his field studies of other people at work in various countries. Ray could do virtually nothing to change the policies his Baptist colleagues had adopted, but he could learn and plan for the future, and this he did with characteristic thoroughness.

Much of Ray's first term was therefore essentially a learning experience but he also made a real contribution, especially in the area of the educational system. The British government subsidized any school that had twenty or more students so the American Baptists were active in teaching and the administration of these schools. We also know that Ray carried out important linguistic work.

He began to look at himself as a Lahu and see his work through their eyes. Soon he realized that the very house in which he lived was a barrier, because when Lahu people arrived at his urban home the first thing that confronted them was a door with glass panels and a doorknob. They had no idea as to how to turn a simple doorknob and in the struggle to open it the door and the glass suffered greatly from their strong, unwashed hands. Everything in the house was a novelty to them. They would examine the food that was cooking and would watch Ray type. They were amused and amazed when a bell rang every time Ray finished a line of type. It didn't take long before they would spit on the bamboo mat that covered the floor, much to Ray's wife's concern. A rocking chair that tipped back when you sat in it would cause them to scramble quickly to safety and sit on the floor. Ray saw that they could never pay attention to the gospel where there were so many distractions, so he and Dorothy began to understand what an advantage it would be if they lived in an ordinary hut like the Lahu and cooked their food over an open fire. The people could wander in, take the fire for granted, and sit in their customary manner on the floor—and spit into the fire if they so chose. There would be nothing to distract them from listening to the gospel that Ray wanted so much to share. It was during the latter part of his first term that his plans began to take shape as to how he would change his methods for his second term.

During his first term Ray spent four years at Meng Meng in the Yunnan Province of China, and while there he made three trips to lower Burma—one of these was to take Dorothy for hospitalization in Moulmein in lower Burma. His last two years were spent in or near Kengtung where Dick was then working, and during those years Ray, Jr. began his education at a boarding school for missionary children in Taunggyi in central Burma.

Both of the Buker families had many contacts with other missionaries on their own stations. When they traveled, they encouraged the Puritan standards by which they had been brought up—rigid observance of Sunday, no smoking, drinking, or card playing. The standards of other missionaries varied enormously, and the Bukers found there was as much latitude in their behavior as in their theology. Ray was careful not to let his many discussions about theology lead to friction because it was the nature of the twins to be tolerant and friendly. In north Burma and in the Yunnan Province of China the missionaries were all solid in their theological convictions, but this was not so in southern Burma. When Ray returned to southern Burma he accurately assessed the theological climate as being liberal and permissive, and even he was surprised and alarmed at the rapid deterioration that took place in the years during his first period of service.

During their first term in Burma the Bukers were frequently involved in discussions with the British officials, and again relationships depended on the individual. One man was so opposed to the missionaries that Ray almost trembled when he received a letter from him. On the other hand, one of the senior officials believed that the missionaries maintained highest standards in both education and medical work. He always supported Dick in his medical work and considered it to be the best and most economical possible. He did not hold these views because of any Christian convictions, but because he was convinced by observation that the missionaries had the well-being of the people at heart and that they were very competent.

In Kengtung state Dick had begun working among the many people with leprosy and soon discovered the advantage of using lay people in this work. He also trained paramedics to work among their own people. He became responsible for the oversight and treatment of one thousand leprosy patients, and was able to give many of them hope for the first time by helping them by medication and rehabilitation. He established a colony for leprosy patients that held about two hundred, but when he conducted a survey of one area alone he discovered ten thousand people suffering from leprosy. This made him realize that in order to treat and rehabilitate such a large number of people, drastic changes would have to be made, and he began to develop other methods that could be used during his second term of missionary service.

For most missionary doctors, the ideal medical set-up is a new hospital with sophisticated equipment and a trained medical staff. Both Ray and Dick came to realize that the more complex the hospital the less possibility the nationals would ever be able to manage it themselves. Their goal for all missionary work was to make the church indigenous, so Dick decided he would pioneer in a public health approach to medical and leprosy work.

During Ray's first term among the animistic Lahu people in the mountains, he heard them say, "Our elders have often told us we used to be a people with a book, but the book became lost. One day a white man will come to give us the book again." This tradition caused the people to respond as the missionaries came to them with the Bible. This type of phenomena is not uncommon and often appears in the literature of cultural anthropology.

The missionary work of the Bukers during their first two terms was in the Southern Shan States (S.S.S.) of Burma and in southwestern Yunnan. Two types of people were found in this area: in the mountains lived more than a score of animistic tribal people; in the valleys were the Buddhist Tai people, the dominant rulers of that part of the country. (N.B. The Burmese word for Tai is Shan. Inhabitants of Thailand, formerly Siam, are called Thai.) Ray also traveled to innumerable villages inhabited by Tai people, who were Buddhists. Missionary work among them was begun by Judson more than a hundred years earlier, and the people had been so unresponsive that the work had been discontinued many years before Ray arrived. The most enthusiastic response to the gospel in lower Burma had been among the Karens. They had not only developed a flourishing ministry among their own people, but had sent out their own evangelists to other tribes in Burma. They had worked among the Buddhist Tai but their results were so discouraging that they reported to Ray and other missionaries that the only way to get a Tai to become a Christian was to take a child and to bring him up in a Christian environment. These then were a neglected people for whom Ray had a concern—a concern so real as to be a burden.

Two convictions began to fill Ray's mind as his first furlough drew near. In his second term he would have to have the freedom to put into practice all the lessons he had learned during his first term from his own reading, observation, and creative mind. To do this he would work among people who had not been influenced by the policies he had inherited and which now he was convinced were wrong and self-defeating.

Ray's second conviction was that the Tai people had to be reached. As Buddhists they were very resistant to Christianity. Their total lack of response was a great obstacle to him, but so what? Nightingale had been a great challenge to him in the Penn Relays. Finishing the cross-country on a cinder track with only one shoe had been a challenge. Chicago Divinity School had been a great obstacle, but he also survived that setback through dogged perseverance. The pastorate of the tottering church in Sabattus had been a challenge, but the God who had used him with such success in Maine was the same God who burdened him about the Tai people. Slowly a definite plan of operation began to form in his mind for his second term of missionary service.

He would make his headquarters in Kengtung, the capital of the largest of the Southern Shan States, and this would be the hub from which six spokes would radiate, each of approximately one hundred miles. In each area he would buy a Tai house, or if that was not possible, he would build a replica of a Tai house. The house would contain one bedroom, which was normal for a Tai house, and the rest of the house would be an open room with an open fire. So when the Tai people would come in they would feel at home. Ray would listen to the people, learn their customs and the way they thought and spoke, thereby becoming thoroughly adjusted to their ways. He hoped and prayed that groups rather than individuals would turn to Christ. What he was planning in the 1930s was what Donald McGavran wrote about in 1954, and was then regarded as a new and revolutionary missionary method. Though Ray uttered these remarks with a chuckle it was perfectly true. The only difference between Donald McGavran and Ray Buker was that McGavran wrote a book on the subject, Ray did not. He wrote it indelibly in the minds of the missionaries he trained and sent to the field when he became the Foreign Secretary of the Conservative Baptist Foreign Mission Society.

That his teaching was effective is illustrated by an incident that happened to one of his missionaries in the Ivory Coast. A group of Christians came to the missionary named Stafford, and told him they had decided they needed a church building for their meetings because the rainy season had come. The missionary agreed.

"We need your help to show us how to build a church," the Christians said.

"Why? You always build your own homes."

"Yes, but we have never built a church."

"Well, build it as you would build a home."

"But our homes are circular, not like a church building."

"Well, draw me a diagram of what kind of church you want," said the missionary.

The Christians drew a diagram of a rectangular building complete with a steeple.

"Where did you get this idea of what your church should be like?"

"We saw a picture of an American church," they explained.

"Who of you will build this church?"

"Oh, we do not know how to build a rectangular building."

"So you want me to help you build a Yankee church?" demanded the missionary. "That is something I will not do. Build a circular building where your people will feel comfortable and at home and I promise I will give you all the help I can."

The missionary told of this experience in a class on missions at the Conservative Baptist Seminary in Denver, where Ray had become the professor of missions. Ray's influence had not been in vain. When Dr. McGavran sought to build the Fuller Seminary's School of World Mission and Institute of Church Growth in the 1960s he invited Ray to become a member of a steering committee to launch the project.

# 7

## FIRST FURLOUGH

As the Bukers' first term of missionary service drew to a close, they began to plan their journey home. Ray had heard of the Round-the-World-Dollar Line, an American steamship company that manned a fleet of liners on round-the-world cruises. An advantage of using this line was that a ship sailed every two weeks, and a person could leave the ship at any port of call, spend two weeks sightseeing, and catch the next ship. Ray had long wished to visit the Holy Land and Italy, and he saw in this arrangement a way in which these ambitions could be satisfied.

There was one snag—the ship did not stop in Rangoon, the logical port of departure. But that was a problem that could be overcome. The party therefore decided to travel to Bangkok, Thailand, and from there to Penang, boarding the Dollar Line ship there. This way they would see Thailand, a country much related to Burma in missionary work. All these arrangements were in character for Ray. The search for knowledge that made Europe so important for him during the Olympics, took him to see the Lisu and Israel and Italy. He never regarded his formal education as a terminus where acquisition of knowledge stopped, but rather a launching pad for new discoveries.

The Buker party, consisting of Dick, his wife and two sons, Ray and Dorothy, and Ray, Jr., set out from Kengtung to Chingrai in Thailand. The first part of the journey involved driving by car to Chingrai in Thailand. After six years of traveling by foot, or at best bumping along on dirt tracks never exceeding 20 mph, they were now able to travel on the newly paved road at approximately 40 mph, which seemed to them more like 70 mph. At Chingrai they changed to a train for the remainder of the journey to Bangkok and Penang.

At Penang they boarded the steamer. It was an American ship and most of the travelers were Americans. Among them was a French lawyer who had been acting as adviser to the Thai government. Ray's breadth of interests and experience challenged the lawyer's and one day he confided that he had written to his wife, "Believe it or not, the most intelligent man on this boat is a missionary."

At Port Suez, Dick and his family stayed on the ship for a direct journey home; Ray and his family left the ship, and traveled via Cairo to Israel where they had a contact in the American Colony in Jerusalem and with whom they stayed. They had a wonderful time visiting the various places mentioned in the Bible, and were fortunate in having as their guide around Jerusalem Dorothy's friend who was a resident of the country. Ray summed up the whole experience as "tremendous." In all these travels Dorothy, who was gentleness personified, entered wholeheartedly.

Following two weeks of sightseeing, they boarded the next Dollar Line ship at Port Said. Disembarking at Alexandria, Ray had an interesting conversation with a guide who offered his services, who reminded Ray that only two weeks previously he had showed him the city. Realizing that the guide must have escorted Dick, Ray tried to explain: "That was my brother you guided through the city." The guide shook his head in unbelief. In a further effort to convince him, Ray pointed to his wife Dorothy, hoping the different wife would prove his point. But it was all in vain for the guide said, "That's all right. Same man, different woman—it does not matter."

Reaching Italy, the family taxied to Naples, over-shadowed as it is by the great volcano, Vesuvius. Here Ray and Dorothy were fascinated in touring the ruins of the once famous city of Pompeii. Moving on to Rome, it was the Appian Way that excited their imagination, when they realized that here Paul trod on his way to ultimate martyrdom. The Colosseum likewise spoke eloquently of the slaughter of countless Christian martyrs whose blood became the seed of the church.

Next was a visit to the steps of Sacra Scala. Here the Bukers were told by a priest that for every step they climbed on their knees, they would have nine less years to spend in purgatory. They looked on with sadness as old and weary women struggled up the steps on their knees. They also recalled that Martin Luther had begun the same climb centuries before when, like a shaft of light in a dark night, he remembered the text, "The just shall live by faith" and he immediately stood up and walked down the steps in a new surge of freedom.

Standing in the ruins of huge pagan temples and then visiting the catacombs, Ray pointed out to Dorothy that while the pagans needed huge earthly temples for their worship, the Christians were content to worship in the simple stark depths of the catacombs. That reinforced his decision to simplify his methods during their second term on the field.

They traveled north, visiting Pisa with its leaning tower, and then on to Florence. This was a city Ray had long wanted to visit because of its abundance of art treasures. It is easy to picture him and Dorothy in their early thirties trudging the streets and galleries of Florence with guidebook in hand. All too soon it was time to hurry to Genoa to board the liner that would take them home.

Each of the twins had clear ideas as to how to use their time of furlough most effectively. Dick had begun to treat leprosy patients through trained paramedics. He had seen that to accomplish his goals he had to do two things that were actually two parts of the same program. Leprosy patients were the outcasts of every society, therefore, when they were cured they needed help to regain self-confidence and dignity. This whole treatment would require rehabilitation, which was the second part of the process. Dick had begun to pioneer this approach but had no other doctor to advise him. He was later to become one of the world's leading authorities on the treatment of leprosy. In preparation for further work in the field, Dick studied for a master's degree in public health.

Ray had many choices open to him, but he decided that he should study for his Master of Theology (STM) degree by studying two quite different subjects, both in the field of the humanities. First, he wanted to broaden his knowledge in socialist studies, specializing in ethnic anthropology, which the dictionary defines as "the study of the races, physical and mental characteristics, customs and social relationships." This was achieved through courses taken at Harvard University with reciprocal arrangements with Andover-Newton Theological Seminary.

Second, he used this period to begin an introduction to the study of psychiatry under the guidance of a seminary professor.

Asked later which of the two subjects, anthropology or psychiatry, was a greater help, he replied anthropology. It not only helped him in his ministry to the Tai people, but also in later years when he conducted surveys of many different countries and cultures to determine the fields in which the Conservative Baptists should work. He then advised missionaries in their work, in cross-cultural relationships.

In connection with his study of anthropology, Ray wrote a paper on headhunters of southeast Asia. His first term had already brought him in contact with the Wa tribe in Yunnan and many interesting facts had been discovered. Although the Wa people were headhunters, they were not headshrinkers; some tribes were both. Ray's main conclusion was that tribes generally did not hunt heads for military purposes but for fertility rites. They believed that to sprinkle blood from a human head on the soil before planting would ensure a good harvest. The Wa in Yunnan had a definite priority in the heads they sought: first, the head of a Chinese; second, that of a Tai; third, that of a white man.

All his research was of practical use to him for he knew that the danger was prevalent only during the rice planting season. Also, that the white man was least vulnerable. Knowing these facts he planned his journeys accordingly. Eventually the British almost completely stamped out headhunting in Burma, and later most of the Wa tribe were evangelized and became Christians.

Ray found that psychiatry proved to be a great help. Back in the 1920s he saw that it was to become a controversial issue between conservatives and liberals. He evidently developed a fairly good grasp of the subject because much later, when he talked to a friend who was writing his dissertation for a Ph.D. in Freudian psychology, he was able to show with some expertise how dangerous it could be to over-emphasize the Freudian school of thought.

In support of these subjects and to fulfill the requirements of his STM degree, he chose for his thesis "The History of the Abenaki Indians of Maine." He knew Maine as a native, having lived in small towns and villages such as Contoocook and Sabattus, where early Indian history could readily be traced.

Working energetically on his research, Ray also paid a number of visits to the headquarters of the American Baptist Mission to discuss problems of the field and to complete his physical examinations, prior to returning to the field. During this furlough year, he spoke at least 360 times, all in New England. This afforded opportunities to discuss theological trends and tensions in the United States with a number of New England pastors. As Ray became aware of the situation in the homeland, he was able to brief pastors on the serious theological problems prevalent on the mission field.

He had always been active in the Student Volunteer Movement and had retained a lifelong interest in students, so he was dismayed to discover that this movement had become very feeble and almost completely liberal theologically. At that time, Inter-Varsity Christian Fellowship had not yet begun its work in this country, and neither had any other student movements been founded.

Generally, the members of the American Baptist denomination did not seem to be aware of the situation that was taking place. Because of Ray's perceptiveness and vision, supported by extensive reading and experience, he was able to point out many pitfalls as he counseled students who came to him for advice.

Among other subjects that had to be negotiated with the mission board was the nature of his second term of service. Ray stated that he wished to work among the Tai people, and initially, the board granted his request. However, their attitude changed when Dr. Robbins, the Foreign Secretary, returned from a visit to Burma where he had attended a large conference of Christians from the Kachin tribe and was very impressed. These people begged to have Ray Buker work with them and Dr. Robbins had promised that he would send him to them.

Ray therefore encountered much resistance. The board argued that after forty years of work among these Tai Buddhists, there were only 100 Christians. Ray explained how his views on missionary methods had changed and he described as an example in detail how his house had been a barrier. He explained what he had learned from Roland Allen's book, and mentioned that on furlough he had bought and studied Allen's second book, *The Spontaneous Expansion of the Church*, published in 1924, and these books coupled with what he was learning in his studies of anthropology, had convinced him even more that his plan was sound and that he should work among the Tai people. He explained how he planned to make Kengtung the center or hub of his work, reaching out in six spokes, a radius of 100 miles each. He would buy or build a house in each spoke, alternating a month in Kengtung, and then a month on out-trips staying in these houses. Furthermore, and basically, Ray and Dick were burdened for the evangelizing of the Buddhist Tai. That there were only 100 Christians was a major reason for working with the Tai. The board was impressed, either by the careful planning, or by his determination—perhaps by both. They granted him permission to carry out the plan he presented.

Having researched and written his thesis on the Abenaki Indians, he now prepared to defend it before an examining committee of three seminary professors. They met in a serious and formal manner and Ray was astonished when the first professor to speak said, "I know nothing about the subject. I have read the thesis, and I am impressed by it and have no questions to ask." The second and third professors reiterated the same opinion. Ray reported that they then had a friendly discussion while he explained that he had carried out his research at Boston Public Library, Harvard Library, and the State Library of Maine in Augusta. The meeting was then dismissed.

Instead of a feeling of relief that would be natural to most people, he only felt frustrated that the examination, for which he had prepared so thoroughly, was so easy. For this year of academic work he earned the STM (Master of Sacred Theology).

Many years later his well-researched thesis on the Abenaki Indians was of value as he became Professor of Missions and Missionary History at the Denver Conservative Baptist Seminary and as a member of the board of the American Indian Crusade.

# 8

## SECOND TERM

As the two Buker families approached Rangoon in January 1934, to begin their second term of missionary service, the contrast with their arrival in 1926 could hardly have been greater.

In 1926 they had been novices in a mysterious country that was full of strange people and bewildering customs. In 1934 they returned to the country of their adoption, a home away from home. In 1926 they knew no language except English; in 1934 they knew the Lahu language and were at home in several cultural situations. In 1926 their destination was Bana, Yunnan, 1,000 miles from Rangoon; in 1934 the destination was Kengtung, a relatively simple journey of approximately one day. The first time they had no plans but to carry out the instructions given by their senior missionaries. Now they had a well-thought-out plan of action to implement. In the first term they knew nothing of the best way to travel. Now traveling in Burma and the Shan States was second nature to them.

They had learned much during their first term of service, but now they regarded that as little more than a preparatory training for their major life work.

During his first term, Ray had worked mostly in China among the Lahu and Wa tribespeople who were animists. Now the twins would work together as a team to labor among the Buddhist Tai nation. The Lahu people had been enormously responsive and the Christians among them numbered approximately 40,000. On the other hand work had been going on among these Buddhists for forty years and there were only 100 Christians to show for all the effort. The twins did not underrate the difficulties before them, but they had made preparations and, above everything else, they believed that it was God's will that they should work among the Tai people.

The Tai were actually divided into five groups, each with its own language or dialect. All were Buddhists. Ray worked mainly among the Tai Hkuin, but used four other dialects: the Tai Hpawng, the Tai Lu, the Tai Neu, and the Tai Yun. These peoples lived in China and Burma and were different in culture and languages from those in Thailand.

At Kengtung itself there was a good base for their work. It consisted of a compound that was divided by a road that ran through the middle. On one side of the road was a small hospital of twenty beds and close to it was a rather palatial two-story missionary home, sometimes called the "Palace." On the other side of the road there was a school with a very active program with a more modest missionary home.

The "Palace" had been built as the residence for the doctor, but Dick preferred to live in a smaller home further away from the hospital. And Ray and Dorothy planned to spend 50 percent of their time in the six village houses referred to earlier.

All of this would involve much work so the Palace was to be the administrative center in which they would live and work for the other 50 percent of the time that they planned to spend at the home base at Kengtung. The remainder of the compound had a series of small houses where the staff of the hospital and of the school lived.

To integrate various types of missionary work is always difficult, and the perfect balance between evangelistic, church extension, education, and medical ministries is never achieved easily and often proves to be impossible. *The Art of Overseasmanship* is the title of a secular book, published by Syracuse University Press in 1957, which is based on a careful study of various Americans who worked overseas. It devotes one chapter to missionary work, but basically it surveys various agencies, private and government, personalities, and occupations. It draws a number of conclusions and recommends what steps could be taken to improve performance levels of Americans serving overseas. One of the conclusions of the book is that the medical profession generally is less successful in adapting to work overseas, both in relationship to local inhabitants and also in cooperating harmoniously with other professional personnel. The Buker team was to achieve a degree of balance and success rarely equaled and never surpassed.

Dick planned to carry on the traditional work of the hospital, treating every kind of disease, malaria being the most endemic. He decided to develop leprosy work which eventually grew from one to ten colonies scattered throughout the State of Kengtung. The colonies varied from 20 to 200 patients each, with an overall total of 1,000 patients.

Medication and treatment administered at the hospital and in the leprosy villages were free of charge, but the patients had to pay for medication that was to be taken home. The American Leprosy Mission was a basic factor in support of the leprosy work, so Dick was able to do his work on the lowest per capita basis of any leprosy work in the world. Development of satellite colonies began as follows: sixteen patients from the village of Mong Pawk made up the main colony. Dick questioned these people and asked whether there were many more sufferers from the disease in the Mong Pawk area. They replied that entire villages in their area were suffering from leprosy. Then Dick realized that with his arrangement to care for a maximum of 200 he was scarcely making a dent in the overall problem. In all, there were at least 10,000 cases of leprosy in Kengtung State and he knew that he had to pioneer new methods.

He created what was, in effect, a junior medical school for the training of paramedics who could staff various outposts for the treatment of leprosy. For this, he was heavily criticized and told that he should use only people with specialized professional training. Subsequent events amply vindicated his system as the right one to cope with the problem.

Occasionally, the patients at the hospital were asked why they did not go to the government hospitals where the medication was free. The reply often was "What, and be carried away in a box?" The Tai people came to see that the Christian hospital provided a standard of compassion and medical care that could not be equaled by the government service and they were glad to pay the small fee Dick charged for his patients.

In the meantime, Ray was also organizing his own plan of procedure. He needed a national to serve as his helper and was most fortunate to discover a marvelous Christian man, named Ai Noi, whose life and training made him perfect for the task. He became an outstanding evangelist and a very important member of the team. He was the son of a Buddhist village head man and as a boy he was accustomed to sitting near his father as he adjudicated the various cases that were brought before him. He trained for the Buddhist priesthood, spending eight years in the monastery. As a priest he wore the usual saffron-colored robes.

One day he fell ill, so he went to the hospital at Kengtung and there was treated by a Dr. Henderson, who gave him some pills. The doctor then said to him, "Would you like me to pray to the God of those pills?"

"Certainly, for it costs no more for the prayer."

Dr. Henderson folded his hands together in an attitude of prayer and prayed for the recovery of Ai Noi. A few days later, Ai Noi saw another priest walking through his village and asked him, "Where are you going?"

"I am going to the hospital for medicine."

"You have no need to go to the hospital," said Ai Noi. "I know what to do."

The priest sat down and Ai Noi folded his hands together as he had seen Dr. Henderson do, and he prayed word-for-word the prayer he had heard from Dr. Henderson.

This fellow priest also recovered from his illness. Because of this experience Ai Noi began his belief in the Christian God. He became a great leader intellectually and spiritually. His Christian training was entrusted to a Karen pastor who had a complete Bible in the Tai dialect, and he and Ai Noi read the Bible from beginning to end with the Karen pastor explaining and discussing as they read. When Noi began work with the mission, he was given the title of Saya, that is Teacher. This was the man with whom Ray worked for six years, and from whom he learned the local Akuin dialect as well as the religious vocabulary for praying and preaching.

Ray secured the houses in six centers as he had planned, and he and Dorothy with Saya Noi went from village to village, sometimes staying in these homes for weeks at a time. At other times they stayed as transients in the homes of the head men of the villages or in the Buddhist monasteries. Dorothy accompanied Ray on most of his trips to these jungle villages.

When Ray and Saya Noi would arrive in a strange village they would be welcomed into the house of the head man of the village. Then they would arrange their bedding mats, Ray would erect his mosquito net, and they would eat whatever food was offered them by the hospitable Tai chiefs. After eating, the elders would gather around the fire in the simple home, with the younger people on the fringes and the women on the outer ring. Saya Noi knew no English or any of the dialects with which Ray was familiar, so after they had eaten, Saya Noi would say, "The big teacher will now teach you." Then Ray would give a brief message using the little vo-

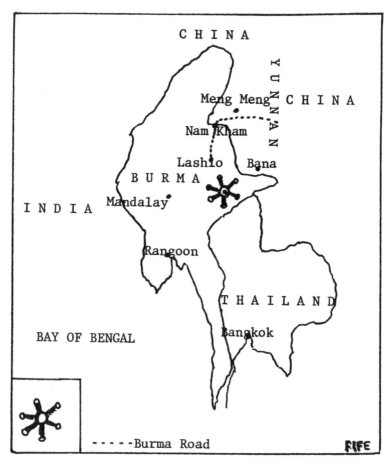

KENGTUNG HUB (see early pages of Second Term)

cabulary he had learned. After Ray finished, Saya Noi would speak, enlarging on Ray's simple message. Using the language of the monastery familiar to the villagers he would discuss with the elders for hours. The people loved it and he would preach not for one or even two hours, but for three or four hours, deep into the night. The people could see Saya Noi and Ray living the Christian life as well as hear them teach it night after night. Often after a couple of hours Ray would crawl under his mosquito net to take a nap. Countless were the nights when he went to sleep with the beautiful voice and teaching of Saya Noi in his ears.

Ray rapidly began to learn the oral language from Saya Noi and from the daily life of the people, applying it as he taught. When he would return home, Dorothy's language teacher would listen to him speak and would say, "His language is terrible, but the people understand him, and they love him as no other missionary I have ever seen."

Saya Noi was an ideal partner for Ray, and as they journeyed together and spent time in the villages people began to respond. Saya Noi was full of good common sense. He used to say to Ray, "People do not come to see a doctor until they are sick. When these people have trouble, they will turn to us and then they will be more responsive to the message we have to give them about Jesus Christ." This often happened and Saya Noi would make the most of the opportunity. "I told you last time how you could avoid trouble through following Jesus," he would say. "Now, listen to me carefully and do not forget the lessons that I teach you and Jesus will keep you out of trouble and difficulties." He would then go patiently through the Christian message, if necessary spending hours to do so. People responded in a remarkable way and Ray and Saya Noi were more and more welcome in their villages to preach and to teach.

All this work was perfectly synchronized, and Dick Buker, Ray Buker, and Saya Noi became a marvelous team, whose training and gifts complemented each other. Whenever Ray would begin a tour, Dick would provide one carrier who would carry with him two baskets full of medicine. Ray would dispense the drugs at each step along the tour.

The relationship between Dick and Ray was surely a unique one in the history of Christian missions. Ray was not only an accomplished teacher and theologian as well as a linguist, but was also a skillful paramedic. Dick, on his part, had learned missionary methods thoroughly from Ray, and since each had identical views on theology with confidence in each other, the program went forward smoothly and with unusual effectiveness.

To illustrate the fact that each was always learning from the other, a couple of illustrations are helpful. Both Dick and Ray practiced baptism by immersion, but Dick had learned that to baptize a person in the traditional way, dipping them backwards, was very difficult in the shallow streams. So he pioneered a new idea. Dignity and respect were essential ingredients in reaching the Orientals, so Dick would have a candidate for baptism kneel in the shallow water and fold his hands in front of him in an attitude of prayer, and then he would bend the candidate forward into the water and pronounce the baptismal formula, "I baptize you in the name of the Father, the Son, and the Holy Spirit." When Ray saw this he realized that it was superior to the method he had been using. For one thing, water never ran down the nose or into the mouth. Also, the position of kneeling with hands folded was a traditionally acceptable posture and as the candidate was lifted to his feet, his exit could be dignified and comfortable, thereby eliminating ridicule from non-Christians on the bank of the stream or pond.

Dick also introduced a method of receiving new church members. When people applied for membership in the church, they were not merely examined by the missionary or the national pastors, but local congregations asked questions of the candidates for membership. Ray reports that their questions were often as searching as the questions that would be asked of a candidate for ordination back in the United States. The people demanded a standard far higher than would normally be expected by the churches in the States and this led to a well-instructed congregation of true spiritual perception and understanding.

With both men working in such wonderful harmony and with such a unity of purpose, it is no wonder that the work began to spread and the Buddhists who had previously been so unresponsive turned to the gospel in ever-increasing numbers, and churches were established.

Dick's purpose was not merely to treat leprosy and rehabilitate its victims into society, but to develop a program to eliminate the disease from a given country. And this was a formidable task. Traditionally the attitude toward people suffering from leprosy was to persecute them and burn their homes, thus driving them into the forests so their illness would not be a threat to others. Dick learned that because of this treatment some people suffering from leprosy would hide it for as long as they could. Leprosy can easily be concealed in its early stages when it is most contagious. Dick knew that if he could only get to the cases early, he could treat them and greatly prevent the spread of the disease. Actually, the leprosy usually burned itself out as a contagious disease after a period of four or five years, and people could live among the well people with immunity. But the chief problem was to find someone who would be willing to undertake this task among such unlovely people.

Ray and Dorothy were perfectly willing to do this, so they went to live in leprosy villages for a week at a time to teach them for their general good. Ray would first negotiate with the local officials for a grant of a piece of land on which the patients could build a village. Then, teaching them to read he would instruct them in the Bible and Christian customs. Soon, mistrust gave way to confidence and surrounding people came to trade with the leprosy patients. After a period of some years, these leprosy villages became the most stable communities in the area, and when war eventually overtook the country of Burma, people fled to these villages because they were the only stable places in an ocean of distress and restlessness.

In his first year back on the field, Ray spent 200 nights of the year away from home working in the villages of Kengtung State. The Buddhists responded to the gospel, and the work of the Buker twins was a partnership that perhaps was unique in the history of missions for it led to a growth of good medical techniques, and also experienced spiritual success in church growth. The reputation of the Bukers began to spread and their work became famous. Among the American Baptists in Burma was a Dr. Seagraves who was heard to remark, "Just think what I could have done if I had been a twin."

Dick himself was to make great advances in the 1950s when he worked in Thailand, but he discovered then that working without his twin was like working with one arm amputated. In all this endeavor, an immense amount of administrative work was needed both to satisfy the requirements of the government for detailed accounting of money and also for the American Leprosy Mission. In the 1950s Dick returned to Thailand, having obtained a second doctorate, the Doctor of Public Health degree, from Harvard Medical School. It was during this period that he held classes for missionaries from many countries, serving with many different boards, training them to take the responsibility as heads of leprosy centers, along with doctors, developing the methods he devised back in the late 1930s which had proved so successful. Dick was recognized as an expert in the detection and prevention of leprosy, although he maintains to this day that treating leprosy does not stop the spread of the disease. Adequate surveys of villages should be made and patients should be treated in the early stages of the disease when it is possible to check the rapid advance throughout the body. By 1950 a new drug, Dapsone, which became most effective in treating leprosy, had been discovered. Dick insists that even today too much of the research on leprosy is theoretic and that what is needed is far more application.

We must mention here that the word *leper* is as obnoxious as the word *nigger* or *dago*, and should not be used. An important discussion on this subject took place in the 1970s. The committee responsible for the translation of the Old Testament for *The Bible, the New International Version* (NIV) was at work when Ray (then in his seventies) asked for an interview—which was granted. He told the committee that the word *leper* was not appropriate to use and he explained why it wasn't. The committee naturally asked for another opinion from an expert in the field of leprosy. Ray arranged for Dick to be present at the second interview, thus affording the committee sound reasoning from the viewpoint of both a specialist in leprosy and a trained theologian. In the Old Testament, as in Burma, a generic term is usually used in Hebrew and refers to a variety of skin diseases. Dick referred to Numbers 12:10 where the *Revised Standard Version* refers to Miriam as being "leprous as white as snow," and the *New English Bible* refers to, "her skin diseased and white as snow." Dick explained that there was no form of leprosy known to medical science that produces symptoms like those of Miriam.

The *New International Version* in this respect is superior in both the Old and New Testaments. Of course there are exceptions, as in the case of Miriam and in Matthew 26:6 where all versions refer to "Simon the Leper." This is evidently because it was used so frequently of this man that he became known by this name. In this case the *New International Version* reads, "a man *known* as Simon the Leper." It is important to note that "Leper" is capitalized in this case as a proper name.

As we think again of the partnership of Ray and Dick, we are amazed at the number of innovations they made in their various types of missionary work. One of the problems they faced at the hospital was that people were frequently coming to the hospital after having been bitten by snakes, which abound in Burma. It was impossible to know which serum to use unless an accurate knowledge of the particular species of snake was possible. Some of the snakes in Burma were poisonous and others were relatively harmless. Dick made a collection of every type of snake and kept them in a pit so that the victims could identify the type of snake that had bitten them. He would then know which serum to give.

As the years slipped by the church grew so quickly that the need for training became obvious in order to produce pastors and teachers. As has been mentioned before, the Bukers were not prepared to send their converts to the established schools and Bible colleges of the American Baptist Mission because of the great inroads made in them by liberal theology.

In facing this situation, Ray and Dick realized the necessity of building their own Bible school, staffed by leaders trained in a conservative theology. This could not be done during their second term, but they considered it for the third term of service. Alas, there was to be no third term because World War II intervened and the Communists eventually came to power in the Southern Shan States. The fruitful years of work among leprosy patients was terminated as the Communists' callous indifference to the worth of human life resulted in the death of these diseased people. Between the years 1939 and 1979, the number of leprosy patients in the world remained fairly constant and is estimated to be between 12 and 20 million. In some small countries the disease is being completely eradicated.

When furlough time came, Ray and Dick decided to stagger their time away from the field. During that furlough, Dick was to work on his doctorate in public health, and Ray would work on his doctorate in theology. This meant that Dick would have to go on furlough in 1939 and only when he returned would it be possible for Ray to take his furlough, but the chaos of World War II overtook them and it proved to be impossible for Dick to return to Burma in 1940.

In 1938, Ray began to notice a lack of energy and he realized he was having some sort of a health problem. He mentioned this to Dick who gave him a complete physical examination and found that his heart, lungs, etc. were all in excellent condition, and he came to the conclusion, although he would not mention it to Ray for some years, that Ray was suffering from "bats in his belfry." Neither of the twins took sufficient note of the fact that they had been working steadily and with very little break for many years, under the most exacting conditions.

With Ray, the situation was possibly aggravated by the fact that on his numerous travels he was exposed to malaria mosquitoes. Although Ray had remarkably good health, troubled only slightly by dysentery, he realized during his second term the debilitating effect malaria was having, even though the use of quinine and atabrine gave a measure of control of the disease. The continued strenuous touring to outstations, coupled with heavy demands of the administrative work, provided no opportunity for the rest he should have had.

After Dick had returned to the States in 1939, other missionaries began to follow him for furlough, leaving Ray with more and more duties. He had some competent assistants, but he was responsible for the missionary work at three mission stations including that at Bana, 250 miles away. In addition to all this, he had the supervision of evangelism and church growth along with the supervision of the schools. These were located in Ting Li and in Kengtung, involving several hundred students. Added to this tremendous load, Ray was responsible for the oversight of Dick's 1000 leprosy patients.

Because the government supported both the schools and the leprosy work, they demanded careful reporting, and although Ray had always vowed never to be a bookkeeper for the government, the work just had to be done and there was no one else to do it.

He was also meticulous in keeping his supporters at home informed about the detail of his work. In addition to sending regular reports to his Mission, and regular prayer letters to his partners, plus writing hundreds of private letters, he frequently wrote features for local New England newspapers. These articles described the country of Burma and its people and the work in which he was engaged. They were of remarkable range and varied from a vivid description of serious damage caused by a fire at a mission station to a hilarious account of his attempt to take part in a cricket match.

Ray was increasingly aware that something was wrong with him physically but he just could not define it. This was not surprising since Dick had been unable to diagnose his trouble, even though he gave him all available tests. Actually, Ray was suffering severe depression. This was caused partly by the side effects of atabrine, which produced a toxic condition, and by exhaustion. This combination brought on a nervous breakdown.

During the war years, Dick also suffered a breakdown, and although compelled to remain in the United States, he worked from two medical offices in the State of Maine. He began to suffer from many of the symptoms Ray had had, and he then felt remorse and guilt for his lack of sympathy and understanding toward his twin. He even felt that it was the judgment of God on him for his attitude toward Ray.

Dick was eventually drafted into the army as a medical officer serving for a time in Brazil. His nervous condition remained the same, and after a time he wrote what he considered a detailed diagnosis of the problem both he and Ray had. He explained that the nerves had protective layers that had been worn away by constant exhaustion and overwork. With both Ray and Dick this was accompanied by insomnia and the various symptoms of a nervous breakdown.

Ray could not sleep at night unless he rested for at least two hours in the afternoon. He thoroughly enjoyed his work, but even enjoyable work can demand a great price. He found that he could work only in forenoons, and after lunch he had to rest, followed by work that to him was very therapeutic. This was the work of translating the Book of Mark from Greek into Hkuin, reflecting his skill as a linguist. He was the only white man who ever learned this language. His life had also become a lonely one; there was no recreation, no diversion, although radio newscasts were helpful in changing his focus. If he accepted a social invitation from one of the British officials involving a late hour, he found it impossible to sleep very much. Only by regulating his activities to insure at least ten hours of rest each night was he able to carry on his normal routine.

Returning to Rangoon for yet another physical examination, Ray was given an electrocardiogram. The assistant doctor who read the chart faced Ray with the serious report that he had only three or four months to live. It upset Ray to hear this, not because he was afraid to die, but because of the uncertainty about what the future would hold for Dorothy and Ray, Jr. That night he could not sleep because of anxiety. The next day he went back to the hospital as he had been asked to do and this time he was interviewed by the chief cardiologist. By a strange coincidence he was Dr. Stallard against whom Ray had raced in the 1500 meters in the 1924 Olympic games. The doctor discussed with Ray his condition and said, "I'm afraid I owe you an apology. The electrocardiogram that was administered to you yesterday was read upside down by my assistant." Ray was greatly relieved because he was now able to consider the future with optimism and hope. Dr. Stallard's report reflected a toxic condition, doubtless caused by the constant use of atabrine. Faced with the need to eliminate this drug from the treatment, Ray found that with only quinine, his bouts of malaria were more frequent, but his condition was less toxic. He struggled to keep his work schedule from day to day, but knew little release from his depression during the years from 1939 to 1942.

Later in life he was to look back on this experience as a marvelous help in enabling him to bring encouragement to other missionaries who suffered similar conditions. But he would never forget the dark days that he had passed through before he eventually emerged into the sunlight at the end of the tunnel of depression.

The mission house in Meng Meng in 1927. This became the Bukers' second home in 1928.

A bazaar scene in Meng Meng.

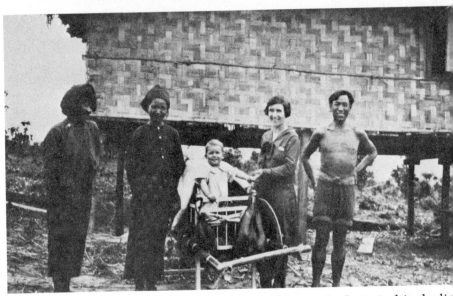

The Bukers' first home in 1927. Raymond, Jr. is in his doolie with his mother, Dorothy, at his left.

Raymond Buker with Ai Noy, a national who became an outstanding evangelist and an important member of Ray's team.

Ray and Dorothy in 1949 at the entrance to their apartment building when he was Foreign Secretary of CBFMS.

# 9

## WAR YEARS

The war came early to Burma, but it came slowly and stealthily. Dick and his family had left in 1938 to take an early furlough. He did this to stagger the furloughs so they wouldn't both be away from the field at the same time.

Burma, being a British possession, entered the war more than two years before the attack on Pearl Harbor brought the Americans into it. In 1939 the British Prime Minister Neville Chamberlain issued an ultimatum to Germany to evacuate its troops from Poland, which they had invaded September 1. The ultimatum he gave to Hitler expired at 11:00 A.M. on Sunday, September 3. At 12:15 P.M., Chamberlain broadcast to the nation from the Cabinet Room at #10 Downing Street, announcing that the ultimatum had produced no reaction on the part of the Germans, and therefore Britain and France were at war with Germany. Actually, the atmosphere of crisis had been rapidly accelerated in Britain for the previous two weeks. On the day Chamberlain broadcast this news to the nation, he also announced that Mr. Winston Churchill had been appointed to the post of First Lord of the Admiralty, a position he had held in World War I. That was almost the only good news Chamberlain was able to give to the nation that day. A signal was immediately sent out from the Admiralty to every British naval unit scattered throughout the world. It was an historic announce-

145

ment, "Winston is back." For years he had warned against the danger of allowing German military might to build up while England was slow and pathetic in preparing for war. The Bukers in Burma noticed that the civilian administrators there were given military status, usually with the rank of Lieutenant. Burma was put on a war footing, although it would be some time before disruption threatened their peaceful existence. Ray now had to deal with military personnel rather than civilian administrators, a task that was often delicate and difficult, and even threatening. The Japanese had been at war in China since 1932, and in 1937 had gradually accelerated the pace of the war in that country, now an ally of the British.

The declaration of war by Britain and France meant that there began to be a gradual influx of Chinese and British troops. Among these British troops were contingents consisting of Indian Gurkhas, who came from Nepal north of India. For generations their only tradition was a military career with the British army in which they had served faithfully and with distinction. Many generations of Gurkha families served in the Indian army, and under specially trained British officers. They were small men, nut brown, and deceptively cheerful in most circumstances. However, when in battle they were one of the most deadly, elite formations Britain possessed. They had fought in World War I, as well as in World War II, causing fear on the part of the enemy wherever they shared in action. Their regular military equipment included rifles and machine guns, but in addition they carried peculiarly shaped knives with carved handles called kukris. In close-quarter fighting the Gurkhas would unsheath their deadly knives and deal with their enemies in ferocious fashion. Their Asiatic and European enemies feared these fierce, courageous, indomitable little men and the cold steel they wielded so skillfully.

Soon after the Chinese entered Burma, Ray Buker established good rapport with the Chinese officers. He cooper-

ated with them and knew a number of the generals of the
93rd Division of the 6th Army. In particular, he was able to
help them understand the customs prevalent in Burma, and
was asked to provide valuable assistance as an unofficial
liaison man between the troops and civilians.

A general atmosphere of unrest gripped Burma, but
strangely enough this proved to be an asset to the
missionary work carried out by the Bukers. In a general climate of uncertainty Ray found that people sought for stability, and they saw this most clearly demonstrated in the lives
of the Christians. Therefore the response to the gospel became greater and greater.

Life grew hectic for Ray, but he was always sustained in
his missionary efforts by the Christian workers and Dorothy,
who shared tirelessly in the work. Their main occupation
was with church development which required preparation of
literature for teaching and training their own church leaders. Dorothy was active in this and was particularly helpful
in working with women and children. Using her small concertina she taught them to sing Christian hymns, and
though not a musician, she was sufficiently accomplished in
the use of music as a tool in the work of evangelism and
discipling. Ray had translated a number of hymns into the
various languages of Burma, and some had been set to native tunes. This was a relatively radical step, for in many
mission fields throughout the world well into the '50s and
'60s, the only hymns that many local Christians learned to
sing were set to Western-style music that was utterly alien to
the local population. Moreover, the words were usually such
a literal translation from the English that they were often
unintelligible to the people whom they were supposed to
help.

From June 1940 when France surrendered, until the
summer of 1941 when Hitler invaded Russia, Britain and
her empire fought the war alone. For at least six months
after Germany invaded Russia there was great doubt that

Russia would be able to survive. Through this entire period Ray continued the many facets of his work but also constantly advised the Chinese on how to understand the customs of Burma and how to gain the most cooperation from the local population.

The tempo of the war in the Pacific accelerated greatly during the latter half of 1941. Prime Minister Winston Churchill had taken steps to send the battleship *Prince of Wales*, one of the newest and most modern-equipped warships in the British fleet, together with a battle cruiser, *Repulse*, to reinforce the Commonwealth forces in Singapore. They arrived at Singapore on December 2, and Churchill was severely criticized for sending two great ships without any escort of aircraft carriers to protect them in the event of an attack. These ships were under the command of Admiral Tom Phillips, and on December 10, 1941, were attacked by Japanese aircraft and sunk with considerable loss of life. When this news reached Kengtung by radio the psychological effect was devastating.

Now the Japanese troops were rapidly invading and occupying largely unprepared countries and outposts of the Allies. Singapore surrendered on Sunday, February 15, and this led to the surrender of 83,000 troops, the greatest surrender in the history of the British forces. As these strategic cities were captured their radios went off the air. Radio Singapore, Radio Saigon, Radio Bangkok, Radio Rangoon—one by one ceased their broadcasting. How deserted the people in Kengtung felt.

Defeat followed defeat. It seemed as if nothing was able to stand before the Japanese army, for it dominated the whole Pacific and appeared to be invincible. They attacked the Philippines, and General MacArthur was compelled to retreat to Bataan. Against his own wishes he was ordered by President Roosevelt to evacuate the Philippines on March 10. And in mid-December 1941 the Japanese began their invasion of Burma.

Ray listened each night to the news broadcasts, and heard about the attack on Pearl Harbor the same day it took place. He told Dorothy, "Now America is really in it." He also added, "We are safe here, safer even than in the USA. Who would be interested in a little jungle setting such as we're in? We are at the jumping-off place from any direction—China, Thailand, Burma." At that time no one could have foreseen that they had but a few months left before they would have to leave, never to return!

Of course, the reaction of the British and the Americans to the news of Pearl Harbor varied. For more than a year Britain had fought alone against the armies of Germany and Italy, and while there were some great successes, generally speaking it was a terrible time of defeat and distress. Under lend-lease America had done much to help, but the British with her allies from the Commonwealth had fought a lonely war.

There had been the disastrous Battle of France, which culminated in the evacuation of British and French troops from the French port of Dunkirk. This was followed almost immediately by the Battle of Britain that dragged on through the whole summer of 1940. During this period the danger of Hitler invading England was constant. In September 1940 the Luftwaffe, under the command of Field Marshall Hermann Goering, launched their furious attack on London.

It is doubtful whether England could have survived those difficult years without the aid of America, but the British were acutely conscious that they were fighting a lonely war against an implacable and well-disciplined foe. It may be difficult for Americans to understand the British feelings when the Japanese attacked Pearl Harbor. Of course, the British were outraged by the unannounced attack and the sinking of the battleships in Pearl Harbor, but at the same time a feeling of relief swept over the British people. They knew at last that they were no longer alone, and that the immeasurable resources of America would be thrown into the war. At last they could see hope on the horizon, even though that horizon was far away.

Ray became alarmed as the major radio stations of the East went off the air. Well before Christmas of '41 he learned that the Japanese had indeed invaded Burma. Although he was in the north, and they were in the south, it now changed everything. How he would have valued Dick's presence during this tremendous period of crisis in his life, but it was not to be. Because of the war situation Dick was unable to return to Burma, and therefore Ray and Dorothy were left on their own. Ray continued to serve as liaison to the Chinese 93rd Divison and they greatly appreciated his help to them. In fact, when they were eventually compelled to evacuate Burma, they wanted Ray to go with them to continue in the capacity of an advisor and consultant, but that could not be.

Curiously enough, the British were so suspicious of the Chinese that they interpreted Ray Buker's cooperation with them as a treasonable relationship. It required international diplomacy to resolve that situation.

One day in talking to the Chinese he discussed the future. Of course, it was not clear either to him or to them what the future held, or indeed if there would be a future, and he certainly had no access to any secret information that would have endangered security. Nevertheless the British objected to Ray's discussions with the Chinese even though he was the one who reported to them that he had had these discussions. He was always perfectly open with his dealings with the Chinese, and he also kept good contact with the British. But the British, largely through the influence of the top civilian officer, Colonel Roberts, decided that Ray Buker should be deported. A colleague of Ray's, Dr. Seagrave, the famous Burma surgeon, then serving with the US 5th Army, was sent to Kengtung to help resolve the matter. Ray reported it to the Chinese generals. Their response was immediate.

"You are now officially appointed as a colonel in the Chinese army, and you will continue to be our chief liaison officer for the 93rd Chinese Divison of the 6th Army." For this position he received a commission but no uniform. From then until he left the State the British could not control him.

Ironically, it soon happened that Colonel Roberts himself needed the help of Ray Buker. A group of American missionaries in Thailand were on the border between Thailand and Burma fleeing from the invaders, and they needed rescuing. Colonel Roberts asked Ray Buker if he would go to the assistance of these missionaries. Ray immediately agreed to do so, and the Colonel gave him the authority to requisition any vehicles he needed to accomplish his mission. He commandeered two buses from the British supply depot and conducted them to the Burma-Thailand border. When he arrived, he discovered that the missionaries were on the other side of the river. A connecting bridge had been destroyed, trapping the missionaries on the Thai side. Ray's knowledge of the people and language once again proved to be invaluable. A raft had to be obtained. Where could he turn for help? The nearby villages seemed deserted, but as he surveyed the scene, he suddenly heard a sound: chop . . . chop . . . chop. Someone was pounding rice. He called out. Hearing a voice speaking to them in their own dialect, some of the villagers came out of hiding, excited to find someone with whom they could communicate. Under Ray's instructions, the villagers were persuaded to build a raft, and eventually paddled across the river with Ray, picked up the missionaries, and ferried them with their baggage to the Kengtung side.

The missionaries had been fleeing from the Japanese for weeks, and were in a state of bewilderment and fear not knowing which way to turn. It was an enormous relief to them to find in Ray a fellow countryman and a resident of Kengtung. Most of these missionaries were Presbyterians, but a few belonged to the Christian and Missionary Alliance. Ray put them in the buses, taking them to his home in

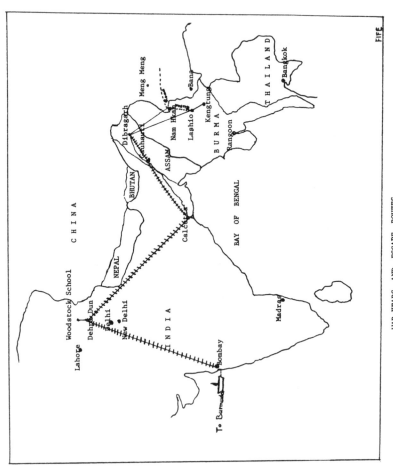

WAR YEARS AND ESCAPE ROUTES

Kengtung, arranging for the sleeping and eating for a score or more of these American visitors. The distraught missionaries found Dorothy a source of strength, for they had not met a person so calm and self-possessed in weeks. In leisure moments, she quietly knit, bringing comfort and encouragement as she shared her heart and home in the midst of confusion and chaos. Much later, in America, these missionaries remarked to Ray what a help and a blessing it had been for them to see the example Dorothy set when they came to her home.

Fortunately, Ray was able to arrange for them to be evacuated to Rangoon before that city fell to the advancing Japanese troops. Shortly after that Rangoon was besieged on three sides by the advancing Japanese, and the commander of the British troops sent a cable to Prime Minister Churchill asking for an army to be sent immediately. Winston Churchill was in no position to send an army, but he remarked, "We could not send an army, but we did send a man." He sent General Harold Alexander. What else could Winston Churchill have done? Field Marshall Erwin Rommell with his Africa Corps was wreaking havoc in the desert war at that time, and the British forces were stretched to the limit.

In addition to sending precious weapons such as tanks, antitank guns, ammunition, and planes (one in four of these were lost by torpedo attack) to Russia, the tiny British army had to maintain military units in Northern Ireland, Iceland, Bermuda, the West Indies, Gibraltar, Malta, East and West Africa, Abyssinia, Eritrea, Sudan, Egypt, Palestine, Syria, Cyprus, Iraq, Persia, Arabia, etc. In fact, the very security of Australia was being threatened by the advancing Japanese through New Guinea, and the Australian government demanded that some of the Australian troops be returned from the Middle East to defend their homeland.

In sending General Alexander, Churchill had sent no ordinary man, but his favorite British general. When Alexander first arrived in India he realized that a situation of chaos existed. The armies in Burma were under the nominal command of General Wavell, who himself was the victim of the absurd administrative machine that made Burma subject to his control in India.

As early as the late 1920s, it had been recommended that the British government sever the tie between Burma and India and administer them as separate entities. But the British cabinet refused to do so. Now Wavell was too far away to be able to control the situation as it existed in Burma, and he ordered General Alexander to proceed to Rangoon to save the city.

But it was too late, for at that time Rangoon was so threatened that it could not possibly be saved. But Wavell suffered from three facts; first, he had to keep the nationalist movement in India under control; second, he was too far from Burma to cope with the problem; and third, he seriously underestimated the fighting ability of the Japanese. He had had enormous success himself in fighting the Italians in the western deserts and in Ethiopia, and he regarded the Japanese as no better than the Italian soldiers whom he had so easily conquered through sheer genius and military strategy. At the end of the war, Wavell was one of few generals, perhaps the only one, to admit that he made an error of judgment in underestimating the capacity, training, and skill of the Japanese army. Alexander had had a very distinguished career in the British forces. In a book entitled *Walk Out With Stilwell in Burma,* the author, Frank Dorn, who was the executive officer under General Stilwell, and certainly no lover of the English, described one scene in which he observed the conduct of Alexander.

> Silence, then the unmistakeable droning throb of aircraft engines.
> "They're headed this way!" I cried out. "They're coming in fast."
> Everyone leaped to his feet, scrambled out to the

open garden, and stared up at the sky. The silver flashes showed that a Jap bomber formation was headed straight for the town of Kyaukse—and us.

Someone shouted: "Everybody get behind the creek bank."

For an instant no one moved, each reluctant to be the first to run. British, Chinese and American officers looked at each other, then they all made a mad rush for the shelter of the steep bank that dropped away from the garden, just as the screaming whistle of falling bombs began to rain on the town. . . .

I peered over the edge of the creek bank, and stared wide-eyed at an incredible sight. General Alexander was casually pacing back and forth in the middle of the open garden. As more bombs exploded in the neighboring town, he paused, stood straight as a ramrod, and turned his head toward the new fires, a defiant glare in his eyes. I looked about, wondering where Stilwell was, and saw him leaning negligently against the porch railing. He was lighting a cigarette with a steady hand, and very carefully shook out the match before throwing it to the ground. Then he stood frowning up at the planes, his shoulders not even flinching when another bomb fell close by. It occurred to me that if they were putting on an act as an example for their staffs, they were doing a good job of it.

Nothing I have ever read leads me to believe that Stilwell was "putting on an act," and it was certain that Alexander didn't.

What General Dorn perhaps did not realize was that this was a characteristic of Alexander since his first introduction to warfare in World War I. His bravery during that war was so outstanding that he constantly exposed himself to shells and machine-gun fire from the German trenches, and he seemed to bear such a charmed life that superstitious men actually crowded around him feeling that they too would be safe in his company. At the conclusion of the First World War, he served with distinction yet again on the Russian Front.

When the British and French were defeated in the Battle of France, Britain tried to evacuate the armies of France and Britain, and they expected at the most to be able to evacuate 45,000 men. General Alexander was placed in charge of this evacuation, and he behaved with such courage and skill that even as the beaches were being bombed and strafed by German bombers he was the last man to step from the shores of France, having been responsible for successfully evacuating 338,226 soldiers. It was regarded as a miracle that a third of a million men had been evacuated while only 45,000 had been expected to survive. While on the beaches of Dunkirk he was having breakfast, and was heard to remark calmly on the high quality of the marmalade that was served him. General Sir William Slim, who served under Alexander and later replaced him, repeatedly complained that Alexander's indifference to danger encouraged others to feel the same way and so caused needless casualties.

Alexander was later to prove his military genius in being the Commander under General Montgomery in defeating Field Marshal Rommel, at El Alamein, and afterward as Deputy Supreme Commander to General Eisenhower in the Battle for Tunisia, and then in the battle for Italy.

The wonder is not that he failed to save Burma, but that he succeeded in evacuating the British army to India. Few other men could have accomplished this, and perhaps no other military career could have survived such defeats.

In February 1942, the time came for Ray, Jr., who was then 16, to return to school at Woodstock, India. Many years later I asked Ray, Sr. how he managed to survive this trip for it took place after Rangoon was in Japanese hands and approximately one month before Stilwell's historic walk out of Burma with the remnants of a broken army. Ray Jr.'s trip was over the same route that Stilwell took, but without benefits of "air supplies."

Ray explained that for his son the jungles and the mountains presented no problems; he'd grown up with them all his life, and was thoroughly accustomed to looking after himself. It was the older missionaries with him who had the problems, not Ray, Jr.

The war drew closer, and Ray witnessed all the horrors of an army in complete confusion, which was harassed constantly by the Japanese from the air and land, and was frequently encircled and had to fight its way out. He saw people literally cut in half by the terrible machine-gun fire from the Japanese planes. It was a sickening experience, but he kept calm during it all.

Everywhere there was complete chaos and bewilderment, which was greatly aggravated by the irregular blackout of news. Every day, all day, Ray had one of his compound workers pedal a bicycle in order to charge a battery that powered their radio. Every night he tuned in to find news of what was happening about the war, but radio station after radio station had been closed down by the occupation of the Japanese. The lack of news was profoundly disturbing and the ignorance of what was taking place led to an atmosphere of confusion.

The Burmese people had no great love for the British who had occupied their nation, but they had even less confidence in the Japanese, who appeared to be advancing on every front and who gave every evidence they were invincible. In prewar planning military leaders had presumed that the jungle would be an impenetrable obstacle to any invading force. All those theories had now evaporated in the harsh events of war. The Japanese, who had trained thoroughly and secretly for fighting such a war, were able to live and fight under these conditions. Much later in the war, extensive jungle training would be given to the allied troops, but that stage was far off and no one could anticipate when or if they would be able to exist and fight in such conditions.

The home of Ray and Dorothy Buker from 1932 to 1942

was Kengtung, Southern Shan States, Burma. Kengtung, the capital of Kengtung State, was centrally located, 100 miles distant in any direction from other cities. It could well be considered the end of the world, the jumping-off place for civilization in Asia. China is north and northeast of the State and here one comes to the last of the walled cities. From there to the Mekong and Salween Rivers, marking the border between China and Burma, the roads degenerate into paths and trails. The old French Indo-China (now Laos) east of Kengtung, had only trails and paths as well, connecting its major cities with Kengtung. Crossing the border into Thailand on the south, however, one is surprised to find a blacktop road leading to the first city of Chiengrai.

The road out of Kengtung westward to Burma proper was a dirt road where cars and buses could navigate over the 8,000-foot mountain ranges at an average speed of only 10 miles per hour. Traveling 200 miles along this road brought you to Taunggyi, the capital of the Southern Shan States. Kengtung had no economic value, no oil, no mines, no teak—nothing but rice.

The Bukers carefully reasoned and concluded that no army would ever penetrate this spot. There could be no purpose, no reason for such an expensive move in such a resourceless place. They decided to stay there to live out the war—it seemed to be the safest place in the conflict that raged around them.

The winter and spring of '41–'42 was perhaps as eventful for Ray and Dorothy as any in their missionary life. On December 12, 1941 the Thailand missionaries were rescued and sent on their way. In February of '42, Ray, Jr., returned to school in India. Then came the bombing on April 13 of that year. Previously, during January, February, and March, 1942, two planes during two different weeks flew over the valley, the first ever seen in that area. Planes had been heard flying somewhere over nearby mountains, but no one had seen them.

April 13, 1942 dawned as any other day; the weather was fair, the skies unclouded. Then something happened that the citizens of Kengtung will never forget. Here is Ray Buker's personal account:

I was taking my morning trip from our compound on the north of the city to the Roman Catholic Mission to the west for the daily rations supplied our hospital unit. We were loading the car. Suddenly we all heard it—the drone of planes; we all knew at once the meaning for rumor and reports had prepared us. The enemy was upon us—up there in the air. Twenty-seven planes in formation of nine sets of three came steadily but surely, probably about 4,000 or 5,000 feet above us. We rushed for trenches that had been prepared throughout the city—just in case.

Jumping into the first one before me, I found it filled with ammunition—a good storage place no doubt, but no place for me if a direct hit should land here. I leaped out and into the next trench. The drone was now a roar; they must have been only 3,000 feet or so high. Crouching in the trench, I could see nothing. I twisted around to see the heavens for I reasoned death could be no different whichever way I faced. There etched against the sky were pencil-like missilcs, falling from the planes. I heard the boom, boom, crash, chump, thump of the explosions down in the town. Passing over, the planes wheeled back and roared overhead again, this time to the accompaniment of machine gun fire. They were strafing the town now! Suddenly there was silence as the twenty-seven bombers flew away.

I ran to my car. No hits had been made on the Roman Catholic hill compound. What about our Baptist mission compound on the north side of town where my wife, a fellow missionary, and our Christians were? The trip back was hazardous.

Streets were blocked by the bomb craters. On the detours we met the walking wounded; we saw the dead; animals badly wounded were staggering around. There seemed to be no harm to the royal palaces, but many houses along the way were shattered and torn. A hundred bombs more or less had been dropped.

Turning into our compound not a person was to be seen. All was as silent as a deserted city. I jumped from my car and shouted, calling my wife's name. Hearing a low sound, I turned. Here they came out of the trenches. No one was hurt. A corner of the school on the other side of the road had been hit. A soldier guarding the trench filled with children had been killed by the strafing, but not one of our Christians had been harmed. Then the parade of wounded and dying began, brought to the hospital by despairing friends and relatives. One hundred had been killed; fifty were seriously wounded.

The raid was over—that is, the planes were gone. They never returned, but the innocent people who had nothing to do with the war, who were not involved in its promulgation—they were so frightened and how they suffered. The world was falling apart for them and for their future!

Ray and Dorothy had retired early to the upstairs screened porch on the evening of April 20. At 9:30 P.M. a British jeep drove up and a voice called through the darkness, "Are you up there?"

"Yes, we're here," replied Ray.

"The radio blackout of the last three days has been lifted," continued the speaker. "The Japanese have broken through the jungle. You must go before dawn, and even then we are not sure we can get across on the ferry in order to turn northward toward safety in the Northern Shan States. The speed of the Japanese advance on all sides makes it impossible to know the precise location of any particular body of troops. Front lines seem to be virtually nonexistent. The enemy could lurk in the most unexpected places."

There was no more sleep for Ray or Dorothy. They looked around their home, facing the realization of what it would mean to leave behind all they treasured, and especially the valuable library Ray had brought with him. A limit of forty pounds per person for evacuation by air was all they could take.

Ray called in the staff of the mission station and gave them the expected news that he and Dorothy had been ordered to leave. The people were broken-hearted. Their love for Ray and Dorothy was exceeded only by their admiration. These were the ones who brought them the Light of Life, to whom they had looked for leadership for years. Now, what did the future hold for them? Some began to weep. He gave to each of the workers monies for a year's operation. Last-minute advice and instructions for the Christians in this time of adversity were shared from heavy hearts. Only dimly could Ray anticipate what their trials and sufferings would be when the Japanese later occupied the city of Kengtung.

To say good-by to Saya Noi was particularly difficult. For eight years they had lived and worked side by side as brothers. Together they had experienced hardships, disappointments, and wonderful victories. It was a farewell that was worse than a bereavement because of the uncertainties before them.

It was 9:00 A.M. before they were able to leave and even then it was a hectic departure.

Ironically, the Italian Roman Catholic priests were permitted to remain because they were the allies of the Axis and therefore of the Japanese, but these priests were distrusted and disliked by the Burmese people.

At 9:00 the Bukers left in their Ford sedan loaded as heavily as they dared. Ray owned a 3/4-ton Dodge truck which he had sent with his driver into the jungle to bring back some national nurses. The jeep which the military issued was used to evacuate the Chinese Dr. Tan who served in the mission hospital while Dick was on furlough.

After one hour of slow travel Ray had a flat tire. He opened the trunk of the car but found to his dismay that there were no tools, not even a jack. At this point, a British officer who was a friend of Ray's, drove up in his small British car. He immediately offered to help Ray change the tire, but when he got the jack from his little car, it was not capable of lifting the tires of Ray's car off the ground. Ray went into the jungle, cut down a tree, and used this to lever the car up to change the tire. The going on Kengtung's roads averaged about 10 mph. They drove for a hundred miles until reaching a place called Mong Ping, which was the half-way point to the ferry. Getting out of the car to unpack the bedding, he found to his dismay that he had another flat tire. A Burman truck driver who spoke no English saw the difficulty, and changed the tire, repairing the inner tube. Ray had no spare by this time.

Eventually they reached the Salween River. The ferry across the Salween had been bombed two days before but repairs had been made and the river was crossed with a minimum of delay. They shortly reached a huge storage depot that had been established by the Army at great expense and considerable effort. Many of the supplies had been brought in by air and would soon have to be destroyed so the Japanese could not get them. Here Ray was able to obtain all the gasoline he had room for. When he offered to pay, he was told that this was an emergency and that people like himself were entitled to unlimited use of the fuel.

After crossing on the second ferry, Ray saw two soldiers walking along the highway who were supposedly Chinese, but he had lived in the Orient too long to be misled. He was convinced that they were Japanese spies sent on ahead to report back to their base as to what was taking place. There was no time to be wasted.

The Bukers' terminal was Lashio, but another night en route was necessary, this time in a native hut. Proceeding on

to their destination with only 25 miles to cover, they had yet
another flat tire. Again, Ray prepared to go into the jungle to
chop down a tree that he could use as a lever to jack up his
car. At that point a British officer and his driver came by,
and the driver changed the tire for Ray.

Lashio was crowded and utter chaos reigned. Ray saw a
bewildering mixture of missionaries, military, British and
Chinese, and his thoughts went back to his first visit to
Lashio in the fall of 1925. The contrast was too painful to be
able to enjoy. They were informed that DC-3's were flying in
to Lashio and that women and children could be evacuated.
It was obvious that Dorothy should leave by air, but the
parting would be hard. Even as Ray drove Dorothy to the
airfield, she knew that he might not survive the war and that
she might never see him again. He tried to reassure her. "I
can probably get a plane later and I can always walk out. The
jungle has no terrors for me and I will walk to India and join
you there." He told her that en route she should stay at
Gauhati in Assam where they had missionary friends. This
she agreed to do, but little did she realize that because of
circumstances, she would have no control over her destination. Flying to North Assam, she found herself a stranger and
refugee along with hundreds of others. Herded onto a barge
on the Bramaputra River she was unable to get off until it
eventually arrived at Tezpur, where they boarded the train
for an overnight trip to Calcutta. The group she was with
were all taken to the Lee Memorial Rest Home and there she
waited in uncertainty. Telephones and telegraph facilities
had broken down. Radios were useless—there was no news
of events back in Burma.

In the meantime Ray drove west and, after leaving
Lashio, which was the beginning of the Burma Road, the
going was easier. He looked back at Lashio only to see great
columns of black, dense smoke, for the British were employ-
ing a "scorched earth" policy, which meant that nothing that
would be of help to the Japanese could be left behind. He

drove on and eventually arrived at Kulkai Kachin Mission Station. A friend and colleague of his, Gus Sword, a missionary with the American Baptists, was in charge of the station. Gus was relieved to see Ray because he was at the station alone.

"What have you done with your car?" Ray asked.

Gus replied that he had sold the car a few days before and now had no way to move out.

At this point both Ray and Gus needed each other on the Burma Road. Ray had arrived on April 25, 1942, so he decided to stay over Sunday to attend the services that would be held in the Kachin Chapel. That afternoon they received a message warning them that it was dangerous to stay and they should get out as soon as possible. They planned to drive in Ray's car as far as they could and then if necessary they would both walk out together. Although he was naturally disturbed by the chaotic events of the past few weeks, Ray had no great feeling of fear since Gus and he had an extensive knowledge of many dialects, and they knew that they would supplement each other. Although many of the people were Tai, the major language would be Kachin.

Their agreement was that they would leave after the church service on Sunday. The news, however, became worse, so again changing their plans they left early on Sunday morning, planning to drive up the Burma Road to Loi Wing (Nam Hkam) on the China border. Again the experience was unpleasant. Littered along the roadside were many wrecked lorries, some the result of bombing and machine gunning, some because of breakdown, but all had to be abandoned because nothing could be permitted to block the road. It was a devastating trip.

Eventually they arrived at the hospital at Nam Hkam, a mission station of the American Baptist Mission. Dr. Seagraves had built and developed his medical work here. However, he had been drafted to organize all the medical services of the American 5th and 6th Armies. So when Ray and Gus arrived at the hospital they found one woman missionary doctor who was trying to minister in these uncertain and grave conditions.

They went over to the British club and there met a party of about twenty people, most of whom were missionaries, nearly all of whom had been fleeing for days before the victorious Japanese troops. The group consulted together and decided the best plan would be to fly to India. The Flying Tigers, under the command of Colonel Chenault, were flying in daily with military supplies, returning without cargo or passengers.

Ray was delegated to ask Colonel Chenault if the missionaries could ride back to India in his planes, since the journey across the mountain ranges to India was impossible. His curt response was "I don't see why they couldn't." How long would this opportunity last? The danger of being bombed by the Japanese was hourly increasing.

The next morning they heard planes approaching. They rushed out to the field, driving their car to the landing strip. Three DC-3's flew into the airfield and, while the engines idled, the crew threw out the supplies. Immediately the group of 20 escapees threw in their luggage and climbed aboard. Ray's car was deserted beside the air strip with the keys in the ignition.

The crew on the first plane rapidly shut the door and took off down the dirt runway heading for the nearest cloud cover. The "passengers" relaxed as well as they were able to in the aluminum bucket seats along the sides of the interior. They had barely settled back when one of the crew came from the pilot's cabin and said to the group, "You may be interested to know that twenty Japanese bombers have just bombed Loi Wing airfield. We are the last plane that will ever take off from that airfield. The other two planes were still on the field." This was a shocking announcement, especially for some of the women whose husbands were departing in the other planes. In the anguish of the moment, several broke into hysterical sobbing. All scanned the skies anxiously as the plane came out of each cloud, but they were not being followed.

The plane flew on over the ranges of Northern Burma mountains, or as they came to be called by the flyers and the military, the "Hump," landing at Dibragah in Northern Assam. Here they were ordered onto a raft in much the same way Dorothy had been; but the missionaries protested the order. They were informed that if they wished to take another course of action, they would have to sign a document releasing the British from all responsibility. This they did. The train journey lasted at least thirty hours and during that time Ray distributed food to the group. They were extremely grateful, for no provision had been made for the trip apart from the supplies Ray and Gus brought from Kutkai. One of the missionaries actually got on his knees to thank Ray for all the help that he had been and especially for the food he had provided.

Ray laughed and asked Gus, "Do you know where this food came from?"

"Of course not. All we know is that you have provided it and it is a gift from God, and we thank you for it."

"But, Gus, do you not realize that all this food came from your own pantry?"

Gus was dumbfounded. It was his food, but Ray had the forethought to take it along in anticipation of what might be needed for the journey. They arrived at the town of Gauhati where Ray had instructed Dorothy to wait. The train arrived at Gauhati just at dusk. Ray searched eagerly among the waiting missionaries for his beloved. She was not there. Seeking news from everyone he met, Ray later that evening received a welcomed report from a missionary who had just arrived from Calcutta that Dorothy had been seen at the Lee Memorial Rest Home.

Ray knew that his responsibility to the missionaries had been fulfilled, so he took the train the next morning to Calcutta. When he arrived at Calcutta the merciless Indian sun beat down and made the atmosphere very oppressive. To make matters worse, fierce riots had broken out between Muslims and Hindus and many hundreds, and perhaps even thousands, were killed. Ray made his way as quickly as he could to the Lee Memorial Rest Home, where he found his beloved Dorothy. It was a joyful and tearful reunion. God had brought them through great dangers and now they were relatively safe together in India.

During the brief time they spent in Calcutta, they worshiped in the Carey Memorial Baptist Church—a famous and historic landmark. Ray noticed that on the walls of the church were many plaques commemorating various historic events and people. Then he remembered that this was the church in which Adoniram Judson had been baptized. While his eyes searched the walls he discovered that he was seated beside the baptistry, and there he discovered the commemorative plaque indicating this was the exact spot where Judson had been baptized in the previous century. For Ray it was a tremendous moment because it was Judson who was the first missionary of the American Baptist Foreign Mission Society and who had translated the Bible into Burmese.

The Bukers' next move was to join their son in Mussoorie, a hot season hill station for central India. Ray, Jr. attended the Woodstock boarding school for missionaries' children northwest of Calcutta. Two days of train travel brought them to Dehra Dun, the hill station at Mussoorie. From Dehra Dun they made their way up the mountains at 7,000 feet to Woodstock School.

Ray, Jr. was very happy at that school, and it had become virtually a home for him as he spent much more time there than he did in Burma. He also had many friends there so he told his parents that he would like them to leave him in Woodstock School until he graduated two years later. Ray replied, "My son, we are a family and in a war many different things can happen. We will stay together as a family and you will come back with us to America."

They waited in Mussoorie for nearly three weeks to arrange transportation to the United States. Such transportation was very hard to come by in wartime, but they were eventually informed that a troop ship would be returning to New York from Bombay and that they could have a passage on it. They would be limited to a maximum of fifty pounds of luggage per person but this mattered little as they anticipated returning to the States.

As Delhi was on the direct route to Bombay, Ray decided that he must make the trip from Delhi to Agra to see the Taj Mahal, one of the most famous mausoleums in the world. It was built in A.D. 1645 by the then ruler of India in memory of his favorite wife who died in childbirth. Ray regards it as the most beautiful ever built by man. He had seen St. Peters in Rome, and he thought that that might be a greater building, but for sheer beauty the Taj Mahal at moonlight he described as being "out of this world."

When the Bukers arrived in Bombay, they made their way to the docks and there they boarded the SS *Brazil*, which had been a luxury liner in peace time and regularly cruised from New York to South America. Now for wartime purposes it had been converted into a troop ship that carried five thousand military personnel. It was about to return to America and the civilians, including the missionaries, were permitted on board. As it had been completely refitted for troop use, there were very few cabins and these were reserved for families that had a large number of children, perhaps four or five. Therefore Ray and Dorothy had to separate and live in dormitories. Ray and Ray, Jr. slept with the men and Dorothy was with the women. Every meal was served cafeteria-style and the passengers had to eat standing up.

The ship did not sail in convoy, which was common practice for fast ocean-going vessels. These ships carried 5,000 men and traveled at full speed without escort, relying on speed to avoid the threat of the German U-boats with their torpedoes.

Strict blackout precautions were in force, and one night a woman standing on the deck lit a cigarette. The captain came up to her and addressed her so forcefully that the officers of the ship said they had never heard a man talk to a woman in such a forceful fashion. The captain explained to the woman that by her carelessness she had made a light that could be seen twenty miles away in the darkness and thereby could make the ship a target for a German U-boat. She was endangering the lives of everyone on board the ship, and it was certain that no one else during the voyage made the same mistake.

They journeyed on in total ignorance of where they were or where they were going. Ray was one of those persons who hated to travel blind and always made a practice of having maps with him whenever he was on tour. He was troubled by the thought that should the worst happen and the ship be torpedoed, no one would know their position, and as the horizon stretched in every direction they had no way of knowing whether they were closer to Africa or South America. Every night he wondered if they would see the dawn; every day he wondered if they would see the sunset at the end of the day.

Ray managed to find four or five men who met every night on the top deck to endeavor to track their day-by-day progress. Maps were forbidden, but Ray had a large world map hidden in his suitcase. One of the other men had some trigonometry tables and they did their best to calculate the longitude and latitude of where they were on any given day. While he was at Bates College, Ray had taken a course in astronomy, and ever since that time he had shown a great interest in the study of the stars and their formation, and indeed had found the stars useful in determining one's geographical position. So this group of men attempted to plot their course from the rudimentary facts at their disposal. Actually, Ray had become very proficient in astronomy and later in life gave many lectures on the subject to interested students. The men had no sextant, which complicated the situation, but they were able to locate their latitude and longitude from the stars. When the North Star appeared it was easy to calculate the longitude. Charting their trip on the world map it was gratifying to find that when they reached Bermuda they were within one hundred miles of their actual position. All kinds of rumors circulated as to their ultimate destination, but they eventually discovered they had arrived in Bermuda. Cruising into the harbor with total blackout, they heard the droning of the planes becoming louder and louder, and at the last moment the captain switched on the lights of the ship, illuminating it so that the bombers would know that it was a friendly ship.

After a brief stay in Bermuda, the ship sailed for New York. Ray with his family and the 1,000 passengers stood at the rail early in the morning watching the approach to New York which was obscured by a thin fog. Suddenly, through the gloom, they saw the Statue of Liberty. After their many trials it was an incredibly beautiful sight. Spontaneously all on board broke into the Doxology—even though there must have been many who were not Christians—"Praise God from whom all blessings flow." Contemplating their disembarking procedures Ray phoned his father who was living in Rhode Island with his sister. It was his sister Molly who answered the phone, and even to this day he can remember the shriek of her voice when she heard Ray at the other end of the line. His family had spent anxious months worrying about what had become of him and his family. The last news they had received was when they were still in Burma. During wartime, many ships containing mail were torpedoed and letters were lost, so word of their progress out of Burma and into India had never been received.

Molly immediately contacted Dick, busy with his medical practice in Maine. They made plans for a wonderful reunion with family. The summer passed quickly in happy fellowship with family and friends from Maine to Rhode Island.

# 10

# TRAVAIL THAT BROUGHT FORTH A MISSION

When the Bukers arrived in the United States on July 13, 1942, they stayed with Ray's father who had retired, and who was now living in Rhode Island, with his daughter Molly.

It had been four years since Ray had said farewell to Dick and his family when they departed from Burma for furlough in 1938 and eight years since he had seen the rest of his family, so we can imagine their feelings when they were reunited. Dick wanted to be brought up to date on the situation in Burma when Ray left, for much had taken place since Dick had left, and he was more than naturally curious about the growth of the Tai church and the sequence of events that had taken place in his absence.

After approximately a week, Ray, Dorothy, and Ray, Jr. went to Maine to visit Dorothy's home in North Baldwin. This period of Ray's life was to be the most critical and decisive of his whole career. When he arrived back in the States, he was forty-three years of age, and he had already decided that if he was to make drastic decisions this was the time to do it. He was experienced enough as a missionary with sixteen years of unusually successful service to speak as a veteran, but he was also young enough to be open to change, and energetic enough to be exceedingly active.

On the debit side, he was still suffering from the lingering effects of the breakdown he had endured in Burma and also the immense physical and emotional strain of the war years. Fortunately, he was at last away from the climate of Burma, and therefore also free from the malaria that had afflicted him since 1926. This meant that he was able to discontinue the antimalarial drugs that he had used for so long. Ahead stretched the prospect of a welcome change and some rest, to be followed by further study.

One of Ray's closest friends on the mission field of Burma was Joe Smith. Their friendship began in 1926 when they sailed together to Burma as novices. They shared many common interests and convictions with identical views on theology. In two matters they varied greatly. Ray was at the most 5'7'' and Joe was 6'4''. Of more significance, Ray's base of support was in the eastern area of the United States in general, and in New England in particular, whereas Joe's roots were in Minnesota and the Dakotas. They had agreed that each would work in his respective area to bring to the attention of the pastors the true situation that prevailed concerning the theological position on the mission field and to attempt to bring about necessary changes. As neither of them had any special connections with the West Coast they would have to deal with that area in due course.

After being in the United States for approximately a month, Ray visited the headquarters of the American Baptist Missionary Society in New York. This was to be a relatively routine visit while he reported on all that had taken place during the war and the situation as it existed when he left Burma. He was given a very warm welcome and naturally he mentioned his plan to use his hard-earned furlough to work for his doctor's degree. The promotional department of the mission asked Ray to postpone further educational studies as he was urgently needed to undertake extensive work in deputation. The missionary program of the denomination had been weakened first by the years of the Great Depression and then by the war.

Ray was especially needed at this time for two reasons. First, his outstanding work, coupled with his conservative theological positions, could help to calm the increasing doubts of the conservative elements in the constituency. Also, when the liberals would hear him speak, they would understand that the work in Burma had been very successful. Ray understood the plan they had for him but he was not ready to devise any strategy. He had been away for eight years so he needed to consider ways and means with his brethren of similar viewpoints. He deeply regretted the idea of giving up his long-awaited work on his doctorate, and he asked for time to consider.

On this particular visit he was told of two telegrams that had arrived for him that morning. One was from Burma stating that a friend and colleague of the Burma Mission had died in India; the second one, from Wisconsin, was far more disturbing, notifying him that the previous day his friend and colleague Joe Smith had died in a Baptist camp in Wisconsin. The blow was shattering. As he made his way back to Rhode Island that evening, he was dazed and bewildered by the unexpected developments that had taken place during those few hours in the office of the headquarters. His first reaction concerning Joe Smith was to feel that without Joe he could not wage the battle against the liberals in the American Baptist Mission. When he arrived home, he poured out his heart to Dorothy and his father.

During the next few weeks as his strength began to return, he came to two basic conclusions. So far as the death of Joe Smith was concerned, he felt that rather than give up the battle they had planned, the loss of this key figure meant that Ray's own efforts had to be redoubled to make up for the loss of Joe. He decided he had to accept the request that he postpone graduate studies and concentrate on deputation work. He began by speaking at once and soon realized that within the American Baptist denomination an uproar had been taking place, and that it was rapidly reaching a point of explosion.

It is not the purpose of this book to give a detailed account of the controversy that involved the American Baptist Convention because this has been done in two books already in print; the first, *A History of Conservative Baptists* by Bruce L. Shelley, and also by a more recent book entitled, *Founded on the Word—Focused on the World; The Story of the Conservative Baptist Foreign Mission Society.* It is our purpose to deal with the policies only as they directly affected Ray Buker and his personal life and ministry.

This controversy was mainly in America with relatively small overtones as it related to the mission field. It was generally confined to continuously increasing outbursts of indignation on the part of conservative Baptist pastors who were to a large extent rather ignorant of what had been taking place on the mission field.

Ray's health returned and soon he was in such demand that he was preaching as much as five times a day. He now entered a period in his life for which he was well equipped through training and experience, although it was alien to his nature. Other missionaries who were conservative in their theology could and did present their views on what was taking place on the various mission fields of the American Baptist Foreign Mission Society, but Ray soon emerged as the most articulate and formidable spokesman. He knew the liberal position inside out from his studies in four liberal seminaries: Chicago Divinity School, Oberlin Divinity School, Boston University Divinity School, and Andover-Newton. He had not only studied at these institutions but he also had a distinguished academic record. All of this helped him present his case. In the years that followed he was often the target of criticism but no one was ever able to deny the fact that he was competent as far as academics were concerned, and also had a proficient career as an active and cooperative missionary. He began to speak out about the situation in Burma.

We have already noted that when Ray went to Burma 200

missionaries were serving with the mission, whereas when he left there were only 100. Now he revealed the fact that while keeping on the best of terms with the missionaries he had discreetly talked to them concerning doctrine and in particular he had sounded them out on their views concerning the Second Coming. He had done this in such a friendly fashion that it caused no resentment and yet he had done his homework carefully. What is just as important, he was able to articulate the information learned from them.

During the winter of 1942 and 1943, he not only talked about these views but he also put them on paper. The following is previously unpublished material:

### POLICY CONSIDERATIONS

#### (Submitted by R. B. Buker)

The following discussion is a consideration of policies which as a worker and member of the Foreign Baptist Work of the Northern Baptist Convention, I consider extremely vital in order that the work may be continued.

In general, I have tried to follow a policy with my fellow missionaries in respect to their and my theological beliefs of "live and let live." I would be happy if that policy could be followed at all times. In this complex life it is impossible. We do not live in compartments by ourselves. All phases of our work intermingle sooner or later. I am a conservative but I work with liberals in matters of education, medicine, and other phases of social activities. We can agree in methods. In theological beliefs we often disagree. Much of social service activity can be worked together regardless of belief. But in matters of education, unless the theological beliefs are more or less in common, there comes sooner or later a clash. This is more acute in the educational work in the seminaries than in the regular schools.

The situation in Burma has troubled me for

years. I have tried to shut my eyes to it and carry on my own work in my little corner without trying to determine the modes of other workers. Development of our work in Shanland and conditions produced by the war coming just at the time of our furlough make it morally imperative for me to seek some sort of a solution.

Before stating these considerations, it may be well to define the term conservative as applying to theology. I use the term conservative in this paper in reference to theological belief as a man who teaches and preaches as well as believes the fundamental doctrines of Christianity. By fundamental doctrines I refer to the beliefs commonly held by the Fundamentalists.

After my appointment as a missionary in 1926, the General Board have sent out to Burma new missionaries, approximately 80% of whom are not conservative as per the definition above.

In the present setup (when war clouds closed the picture), the students of the three seminaries at Insein were not receiving conservative teaching from our missionary staff.

These two facts present a very serious situation as considered by the conservative, whether a missionary on the field, a pastor here at home, or a member of the Northern Baptist Convention. From my own personal viewpoint as a worker in Burma, the future looks uncertain and something should be done to give assurance for the future.

From my viewpoint: 1. In the next decade it will be necessary to appoint new missionaries to work in the Shan States. What is there to guarantee that we will have mutual minded co-workers? Under the present setup of the Officer's Council and Board being predominantly liberal, is there any honest assurance that in the future we will have conservative co-workers in Burma? 2. By nature of developments in the Shan States, the co-workers with the Baptists are the conservative Bible Churchmen's Missionary Society. Their number is increasing. They are willing to cooperate with conservative Baptists. What assurance can we give them that we will appoint such workers? 3. I have had to come to the decision that we cannot send any of our Shan boys to the liberal seminaries of Insein. I am accused of noncooperation, when really the liberals have so dominated the situation that the conservatives have no alternative but to withdraw. The Bible Churchmen's Missionary Society will have nothing to do with the liberal seminaries at Insein. What can be done to rectify this situation?

From the viewpoint of the conservative constituency: In recent years the missionary setup abroad has been represented to the constituency as being essentially conservative with some liberal elements. Aside from one or two fields such as Assam, I consider this presentation as false. The setup is essentially liberal with some conservative elements.

Conservative missionaries now in America are asked to deputate among all churches which have varying shades of attitudes on this problem. That is, we are encouraged to present the missionary situation on the field as essentially conservative. Even though we say nothing orally directly about this matter, our very presence and account of our work is supposed to leave the impression that all our missionary program on the field is essentially as we have described. This I consider as subtle, dishonest, and almost hypocritical. The recent change in the Officer's Council tends to aggravate the whole situation. Conservative groups are fast losing confidence in our denominational foreign mission setup. If we continue trying to cover up our liberal positions, the eventual result will be a serious breaking away of the conservative churches in our denomination.

If the Board and Officer's Council are to take the position, "We are very sorry. We do not wish any

break in our denomination. We wish the conservatives would work with us. But we cannot change our
position," then it is only fair to ask the conservative
missionaries who wish to represent and to work
with and for our conservative Baptists to make some
arrangement that will enable them to feel free and
honest to do this thing. Otherwise, there should be
some adjustment in the present situation.

After presenting this statement to the American Baptist
Foreign Mission Society Ray was urged to circulate it among
some thirty very influential pastors throughout the eastern
part of the country. Subsequently, at a meeting at Grace
Baptist Church in Philadelphia on May 18, 1943, it was accepted as a basis for formal recommendation to theologically
conservative Baptists. These were as follows:

Adopted by The Baptist Christian Fellowship of
Philadelphia:

WHEREAS:    The division of the Missionary Enterprise into Conservative and Liberal groups has created innumerable
problems, and

WHEREAS:    Conservative individuals, churches,
and groups have ceased to support
our Missionary Program, and

WHEREAS:    There is widespread indifference
and lack of information on the part
of many conservative-minded individuals, churches, and groups, and

WHEREAS:    We feel that information concerning
these matters should be as widely
disseminated as possible,

THEREFORE:    BE IT RESOLVED that we, The Baptist Christian Fellowship of the
Philadelphia Area request our State
and National Fellowships respec-
tively to make a careful study of the

following resolutions, and endeavor to secure a widespread dissemination of knowledge of such a proposition, namely:

1. That the conservatives of the Northern Baptist Convention will select representatives to promote definitely conservative missionary work in personnel and field within the Foreign Missionary Program of our denomination;

2. That they shall arrange for certain definite areas of Missionary service which shall be unmistakeably Conservative in order to facilitate the designation of Conservative money for Conservative work.

Adopted in a meeting at the Grace Baptist Church, May 18, 1943. Committee consisted of:

Rev. Harold Oyer,
Rev. Samuel Jeanes,
Rev. Ellwood Schaumberg.

Respectfully,

Ellwood E. Schaumberg,
Secretary

At the time this was taking place, Ray was in demand over a greater geographic area. He went from New England and the East Coast to the Midwest, and then did extensive deputation work even on the West Coast.

As is often the case when disagreement has been circulating for a number of years, it took one particular step to bring matters to a head. In February 1943 a new foreign secretary of the Foreign Mission Board, Elmer A. Fridell, was appointed. Dr. Fridell tended to be, perhaps intentionally, vague about his theological views, but he was generally regarded by the conservatives as being theologically liberal. His appointment triggered an enormous explosion. Dr. Richard Beal, pastor of the First Baptist Church of Tucson, Arizona, and a member of the General Council of the American Baptist Convention, sent a telegram to the American Baptist Foreign Mission Society. In this telegram he stated that the reaction of his church to this appointment was that they would withhold all contributions to the ABFMS until the Board rescinded the election of Dr. Fridell. He also sent copies to many conservative pastors within the Convention including Dr. Albert Johnson, pastor of Hinson Memorial Baptist Church in Portland, Oregon, who also reported that the ABFMS would receive no further gifts from his church unless the new secretary resigned.

One leading pastor wrote, "We cannot help realizing that we have lost something vital when the records of our foreign missionary society show that in 1923 we had 845 foreign missionaries and today we have 434 or nearly fifty percent less. In 1923 our missionary giving for foreign work was $1,079,343; last year it was $499,982, or a fifty-four percent decrease." The downhill slide of the mission is revealed in those few statistics and the significance is plain to see.

On May 18, 1943, while all this was going on, Ray received an honorary Doctor of Divinity degree from Eastern Baptist Seminary in Philadelphia and the following previously unpublished citation was read.

## CITATION

Mr. Raymond Bates Buker was born in Rhode Island, the son of a Baptist Pastor. He received his A.B. degree from Bates College, his S.T.B. from Boston University School of Theology, and his S.T.M. from the Newton Theological Institute.

Following a successful pastorate, Mr. Buker was commissioned by the ABFMS as missionary to the Lahu and Wa in Yunnan and Kengtung, Burma, in 1926, where he served until 1931.

After his furlough, he organized a leper colony among the Lahu and ministered to the Shans in Kengtung, where he served until forced to return home on account of the war. Mr. Buker has published a 40-page Catechism in Lahu and the Gospel of John in Hkuin. This Gospel of John is the first published document, Christian or otherwise, in the Hkuin language. He has also completed the translation of the Gospel of Mark in Hkun, and this is in manuscript awaiting publication.

Mr. Buker is a successful evangelist, soul-winner, and true Christian missionary statesman.

Mr. President, by vote of the Board of Trustees and with the recommendation of the Faculty, I am glad to present Mr. Raymond Bates Buker to receive at your hand the degree of Doctor of Divinity in recognition of his distinguished service as a Christian minister.

In July of 1943 Ray Buker received an invitation from Dr. Gordon Palmer, the president of Eastern Baptist Seminary, to join the faculty of that institution. A letter dated July 9 from Dr. Palmer reads as follows:

Box 7653
Philadelphia 1, PA
July 9, 1943

Dear Brother Raymond,

I can't get away from the idea of having you connected in a vital way with Eastern. Every door seems to have shut against me in getting the right man for the successor to Dr. Livingston in the Chair of Evangelism. I am going to lay before you what I think is a great opportunity for service for God's man. If you should be at all interested in this position after you have read my statement write me and I will have you come down to talk over the situation with me and then I will get the Committee together and have you appointed if a mutual satisfactory arrangement can be agreed upon. You have been constantly in my mind since our first meeting. . . .

The man who has held this position has worked with me in representing the seminary at the state and national conventions and in the churches because he has then been able to guide pulpit committees to some of our men. . . .

I have prayed and thought and thought and prayed and I cannot get away from you. If the missionary doors should close for you it is quite possible you would find this appealing to your heart, mind and soul. I earnestly pray that you may be led to give this serious and I trust favorable consideration.

If the LORD IS IN THIS HE WILL REVEAL HIS WILL CLEARLY TO YOU AND IF WE ARE LED BY HIM HE WILL MAKE THE DECISION UNANIMOUS ON THE PART OF OUR BOARD. Then I know you would be exceedingly happy in this new fellowship no matter how difficult the work or the days ahead. . . .

God bless you and your wife and family. I have had to be away from my office for the past few days and will be home again next Saturday. I shall be awaiting your reaction with great interest and in much prayer.

Yours most cordially,

Gordon Palmer

Ray received a second letter from Dr. Palmer dated July 21.

Gordon Palmer
1305 Medford Road
Wynnewood, PA
July 21, 1943

Dear Doctor Raymond,

I was glad to get your postal. I was afraid you had decided to put it aside and forget it. But it does give me a little hope that you may feel the Lord leading in this, just as we do. I am confident that the Board would be unanimous in electing you to this position and I also am confident that the Faculty would be unanimous in their approval and support.

It has been on my mind ever since I wrote you two weeks ago and have been earnestly praying that God will make it clear that you will be definitely interested in this opportunity. If you want to be where you can influence young people for Christ and for the basic truths of the Bible and in missionary and evangelistic endeavor this is the greatest place open to anyone.

If you are at all interested, be sure to wire me so that we can arrange a conference at the earliest possible date as we do want to get something going in this department before September first. I have not approached anyone else since the Board made a request that we get a man of your type for this work. If, of course, you are not interested and that there is no possibility of persuading you to seriously and favorably consider this kind of work, I must know so that I can follow other leads. You, I am confident, are the first choice of any prospects we have. So I do not want to move toward any other until I know it's no use trying to persuade you to come to this fine place and challenge. Wire me collect and let me know the date I could see you to go over this with you. I will see that your expenses are provided for if there is any hope at all. When you come down, I think you had better make it so that I could get as many of the committee as possible present to confer with you also. Then, we can call an Executive meeting to make the call official.

God bless you, my friend.

Pray much for guidance in this for we want His will to be done.

Yours most sincerely,

(signed Gordon Palmer)

Ray replied to these letters as follows:

North Baldwin, Maine
July 27, 1943

President Gordon Palmer
1305 Medford Road
Wynnewood, Pennsylvania

Dear Dr. Palmer:

Your letters of July 9th and the 21st are before me. I will summarize my answer in this first paragraph and then go on to detailed explanations. I do not yet feel the leading of God to give up foreign missionary work among the Shans. I am asking Him that if it be His will to make it very clear indeed. I know the needs of Shanland. He has revealed these needs to me, and it becomes an added responsibility to me to keep these needs clear and defined.

Your offer to work in Eastern strikes a very, very responsive chord in my heart, soul, mind, and body. I know of no other situation in America where I personally would prefer to work. My first choice would be Missions. But after all Missions is only a branch of Evangelism. My interest and passion certainly include any phase of Evangelism. Personally I would be most happy in every phase of the work you outline, teaching of Missions, of Evangelism, organizing and promoting the work of the students among the churches, etc. So far as the financial arrangements were concerned you did not need to write me. If the Lord calls me to a position I am sure the wherewithal will be sufficient.

But I cannot accept the offer—not now—not yet. 1. Altho my wife and I have had one leading that our work in Burma may be closed (please keep this confidential) it is not yet sufficiently clear for us to believe it is a fact. We are waiting the closing of the doors by Him. I do not consider an offer in another place as closing the door, it merely opens the door in another way—and now we are having many offers here and there, but none appeals as does the Eastern opening. You may be assured that if we take any work Eastern will have first consideration.

2. We should consider most carefully if I am really qualified for this position. There is no doubt as to my interest, enthusiasm and passion for evangelism. But do I have the background and experience for this work. For the first few years I might make a bit of a splurge, but unless I have something very durable I might become a drag to Eastern. As I conceive the position it should have a man with considerable experience in evangelistic work and among the churches of America. What have I? I was 10 months in a rural pastorate in Maine. In that time we tripled the membership—from 20 to 60, 21 by baptisms. My only "evangelistic campaign" as such is the one just completed at the Baptist School for Christian Leadership. I preached and gave the invitation every night, with results, but this was not in a church at that. My qualifications to advise in church problems are limited to my experiences in a minister's family—four pastorates of my father and a more or less extensive traveling among churches as a deputator for the Foreign Missionary Society. . . .

Certain positions as attractive as this one I would be keen to try for a year or so, knowing when I began that after that time the way to return to Burma might open. But with the particular position you have offered it is obvious that for the first two or three years I would not be worth too much. Those first years are only preparatory to a fruitful life work. There would be months of exceedingly concentrated study to get the courses lined up. These first years would be the introduction in learning the situation in the local churches where we are asked to advise and help. Only after this introductory stage would I be at my best in terms of service to the institution and the work as a whole. And yet in the next two years I will be in the most demand throughout the denomination to present the missionary challenge. For these reasons therefore I have not played with the idea of accepting the position as a temporary matter for one or two years. . . .

I understand and agree that the influence I might have in the Seminary might be greater in its wide applications than just being a missionary to the Shans. But I feel God has chosen me for the Shans. It would take 10 years for a man to reach the position of usefulness that I can be for that country. I know two languages of the area as well as the background and set up. I cannot walk out on them in this their time of travail—I could never challenge young people for this kind of service until and unless God shuts the door to me. There are men already trained and with the same qualifications as myself in America who can do the work at Eastern. Only the Youngs and the Bukers are trained to do work among the Lahu and Shans. . . .

To Summarize and conclude: At present we do not see that God has closed the door for us to work in Shanland. This releases you from any obligation in your offer to me. You will continue to look for someone to fill the position. If you find a man, all well and good. However, if at the end of a year, or at any time when I feel God has closed the door to our working in Shanland, I will certainly inform you and if there is an opening I will be exceedingly happy, personally, to be associated in the work at Eastern. . . .

> Very sincerely yours,
>
> (signed Ray Buker)

(Again, this is formerly unpublished material.)

These two letters, plus the Citation read at the time Ray received his D.D., speak of the high esteem an influential leader such as Dr. Palmer had of Ray Buker. Ray's reply reveals his determination to continue the work among the

Shan or Tai people of Burma and was a carefully reasoned account of why he should not accept a position in a seminary at that time.

There are a number of things in these letters that are intriguing, but one in particular is typical of Ray Buker's attitude toward his own gift for evangelism—or lack of it. At the beginning of his letter he mentions how God had blessed his efforts in evangelistic activity in a conference at North Aroostook and yet goes on to take the view that he had no true evangelistic gift. This was a view that obviously was not shared by Dr. Palmer or the faculty of Eastern Seminary. For the rest of Ray's life he continued to declare publicly that he possessed no evangelistic gift, an opinion that flies in the face of much evidence both in Burma and the States. He was and remains a man who seriously underestimates his own gifts and accomplishments, and this citation was one that gave ammunition to his enemies later.

Ray's letter also reveals at least three other significant details. First, it mentions how his prime concern was that the good name of Dr. Palmer and the seminary might be endangered by his inadequacy; second, it reveals his continued determination to be true to his missionary call; third, there is the hint that he already had some indication that his further work in Burma might be impossible. At this stage the war in Burma appeared to have been won by the Japanese, and Ray's letter of July 27, 1943 was written before the successful counter invasion by the American, Chinese, and British troops had been launched.

To many men of Ray's age this invitation would have been an offer so attractive as to be almost impossible to refuse. The security that such a position offered, together with the opportunity for a widening ministry and a position of growing status, did not for a moment change his attitude to what he considered to be the vital priorities.

During the fall of 1943 the cry for another mission board was heard more frequently. Dr. Kenneth Scott Latourette was the Professor of Missions and Oriental History at Yale Divinity School, and the author of the monumental seven-volume *History of the Expansion of Christianity.* He was also the Chairman of the Board of the ABFMS. The ABFMS knew that Ray had enormous respect for the work of Latourette and arranged for the two of them to have a discussion which they hoped would influence Ray to remain with the mission society. Ray accepted an invitation to dine with Dr. Latourette and regarded it a great privilege.

Dr. Latourette was warm and friendly. He knew about Ray and his work and questioned him with great interest. Ray explained that he had read every volume written by Dr. Latourette and specifically mentioned that he was impressed by the extensive bibliography in each volume including many which were also published in foreign languages. Ray went on to say, "I presume that you use some of your graduate students as research assistants for your resources."

"No, Raymond, I have read every source myself, whatever the language."

Ray was understandably impressed. Dr. Latourette began to question Ray about his future work and the possibility of a new mission being started. Ray reported that suddenly Dr. Latourette seemed to remember that he was supposed to dissuade him from taking such a step and he leaned over to him and said, "Raymond, we need you in the ABFMS." After that brief comment he continued his animated and warm discussion about missions in general.

Dr. Latourette taught in one of the most liberal seminaries in the country but he never forsook his own conservative and godly views. In the last decade of his life, Dr. Latourette was asked what he considered to be the most important doctrine. He replied, "The second coming of Jesus Christ." Ray was invited to speak at Yale some years later and Dr. Latourette said to Ray as they went to supper, "I do not know what your subject is tonight, but I hope that you will stress the importance of prayer."

Ray was deeply impressed by Dr. Latourette's personality and work but it did not change his mind concerning the problems of ABFMS—in fact, it perhaps reinforced his convictions.

Two possibilities had to be considered. The first was that the conservative members of the American Baptist Convention should resign and join the General Association of Regular Baptists (GARB). This course was not without its problems, however, for though the GARB were certainly conservative in their theology they were also rigid in their attitude of strict separation toward other movements. For example, they were opposed to ecumenical evangelism as would be exercised some years later by the Billy Graham Association. Most of the conservative men in the American Baptist Convention were premillennial, but by no means were they all pretribulationists. Neither were they belligerent in their call for a clear separation from all other evangelical groups.

Ray circulated a paper entitled "Policy Considerations" the previous winter which shows that he had been very impressed by the work of the Bible Churchmen's Missionary Society in England. He had first become acquainted with their group on the ship sailing to Burma in 1926 and later had worked in fellowship with them there. The BCMS was a British missionary society, and its members belonged to the Church of England. They were founded because the existing Church of England (Episcopalian) mission was at that time very liberal in its theology. Ray was intrigued by the concept that it was possible to have two mission boards with varying theological positions belonging to the same denomination. Now in America he and many others felt that this would be the most desirable solution for the split that was threatening to take place in the American Baptist Convention. Actually, Ray and others not merely envisioned two missions but foresaw a possibility that the two missions might work separately in one mission field. For example, the American Baptist Foreign Mission might work in Lower Burma, while the Conservative Baptist Foreign Mission might operate in Upper Burma.

A group of influential pastors consisting of ministers from all sections of the Northern Baptist Convention met together at the Tabernacle Baptist Church in Chicago on December 15, 1943, and voted to incorporate as a new mission organization, the Conservative Baptist Foreign Mission Society with the following Doctrinal Statement:

## DOCTRINAL STATEMENT

### 1

We believe that the Bible is God's Word, that it was written by men divinely and uniquely inspired, that it is absolutely trustworthy and has supreme authority in all matters of faith and conduct.

### 2

We believe in God the Father, Creator of Heaven and earth, perfect in holiness, infinite in wisdom, measureless in power. We rejoice that He concerns Himself mercifully in the affairs of men, that He hears and answers prayer and that He saves from sin and death all who come to Him through Jesus Christ.

### 3

We believe in Jesus Christ, God's only begotten Son, conceived of the Holy Spirit, born of the Virgin Mary, sinless in His life, making atonement for the sin of the world by His death on the cross. We believe in His bodily resurrection, His ascension into heaven, His high priestly intercession for His people and His personal, visible return to the world according to His promise.

### 4

We believe in the Holy Spirit, who came forth from God to convince the world of sin, of righteousness and of judgment, and to regenerate, sanctify and comfort those who believe in Jesus Christ.

### 5

We believe that all men by nature and by choice are sinners, but that "God so loved the world that He gave His only begotten Son, that whosoever believeth in Him should not perish, but have everlasting life." We believe, therefore, that those who accept Christ as their Lord and Saviour will rejoice forever in God's presence and those who refuse to accept Christ as Lord and Saviour will be forever separated from God.

### 6

We believe in the Church—a living, spiritual body of which Christ is the Head and of which all regenerated people are members. We believe that a visible church is a company of believers in Jesus Christ, buried with Him in baptism and associated for worship, work and fellowship. We believe that to these visible churches were committed, for observance "till He come," the ordinances of baptism and the Lord's Supper; and that God has laid upon these churches the task of persuading a lost world to accept Jesus Christ as Saviour and to enthrone Him as Lord and Master. We believe that human betterment and social improvement are essential products of the Gospel.

### 7

We believe that every human being is responsible to God alone in all matters of faith.

### 8

We believe that each church is independent and autonomous, and must be free from interference by any ecclesiastical or political authority; that, therefore, Church and State must be kept separate as having different functions, each fulfilling its duties free from the dictation or patronage of the other.

This historic December meeting which brought the Conservative Baptist Foreign Mission Society into existence, at the same time appointed as their first missionaries Dr. and Mrs. Eric Frykenberg. The Frykenbergs had served with the American Baptists in India with great distinction for a number of years. At last a mission board had come into being such as Charles Spurgeon in England had called for as early as 1887.

When this historic meeting took place, creating the CBFMS, Ray was busy preaching on the West Coast. He returned home for Christmas, and in January 1944 resigned from the American Baptist Foreign Mission Society, but not from the American Baptist Convention. He still had strong hopes that the one convention might sustain two different mission boards and he was by no means alone in this thinking. The idea of the two mission boards belonging to the American Baptist Convention was recommended to that body by the conservatives, but was rejected by the Convention authorities. Strangely enough, within a few months the old Convention was calling on the conservatives for just that action, but by that time they had so enjoyed their freedom from liberalism that there was no turning back from their decision and a break with the American Baptist Convention was inevitable. Of course, as soon as Ray resigned from the American Baptist Foreign Mission Society he joined the Conservative Baptist Foreign Mission Society. It is important to note that his father was strongly in favor of the step he took, as was his twin brother, who was very outspoken in his views that such a movement was long overdue. This was an encouragement to Ray, but in taking this step he forfeited his pension rights from the Ministers and Missionaries Benefit Board. When he eventually retired he received only the amount that had accrued prior to 1944.

The CBFMS held its first annual meeting in Atlantic City on May 22, 1944, and seventeen candidates, including Dr. and Mrs. Frykenberg, Dr. and Mrs. Raymond Buker, and Dr. and Mrs. Lee Lovegren, former members of ABFMS, were formally appointed. The new society set up its offices at 185 N. Wabash Street, Chicago, and its first general director was Dr. Vincent Brushwyler, who died in 1980. Since Ray Buker was not able to return to Burma, he was appointed as the first Overseas Secretary, a role that was to continue until 1956.

Although the number of pastors and missionaries withdrawing from their denomination was large, and included men of great stature and influence, it was inevitable that some who had been critical for many years could not face the trauma of a final break, so remained within the Convention. Ray's early projection for a new mission society was modest indeed. If five couples could be appointed with a support figure of approximately $4,000 each, it would form an adequate nucleus. The basic purpose was to establish a missionary group with common theological convictions that could work harmoniously together establishing churches and training leaders, all holding a similar theological stance. It would have boggled the minds of those trailblazers if they could have realized the growth and size of the CBFMS thirty-five years later, with more than 500 missionaries with an average annual cost per couple exceeding $20,000, and with an annual income of more than ten million dollars.

# 12

## FOREIGN SECRETARY

The actual invitation to become Foreign Secretary of the society was given to Ray in the CBFMS headquarters on the ninth floor on Wabash Street in Chicago. He walked to the window and looked out into the darkness while he considered the offer. After a few minutes he turned and spoke. "I hate administration. I long to do the work of a missionary on the field. I would sooner jump through that window than be an administrator tied to an office. Nevertheless, I cannot get a visa for Burma at this time, and I see the urgent need for a Foreign Secretary, so it is my duty to accept this position with the understanding that if Burma opens up, I will return to the field."

Ray Buker had first lived in Chicago while spending one year there in seminary. When he left that city in 1923 he hoped and expected that he would never live there again. Now he faced a combination of two distasteful situations: first, working in an office, and second, living in Chicago. But he reacted as he did to every new challenge and duty in his life—he simply gave all of himself to the task of building an entirely new mission from the foundation up. He threw himself into the venture with the self-disciplined thoroughness he had shown in his athletic career. Indeed, he knew no other way—and the growth and stability of the society across the years testified to the soundness of his leadership.

Ray moved to Chicago in June 1944, approximately the same time the Allied Forces were launching their attack on the German Empire at Normandy. He bought a co-op apartment in Evanston, north of Chicago, involving a twelve-mile trip daily to the Wabash Avenue office. After the uprooting of the family from Burma, Ray, Jr. was now attending boarding school at Storybrook, Long Island, New York.

The task of organizing the new mission fell on Ray Buker and Dr. Vincent Brushwyler, who had been pastor of the First Baptist Church of Muscatine, Iowa. It is impossible to imagine two men whose personalities, appearance, and conduct were in such striking contrast. Brushwyler was the General Director and, as such, was the main authority in the new mission; Ray Buker was the Foreign Secretary and, therefore, reported to Brushwyler. In effect, however, they formed a close team and worked together harmoniously.

Policy was decided by a board of pastors, who met three times a year, and who came from all sections of the country. The administration of the policy was in the hands of Vincent Brushwyler as General Director, Ray Buker as Foreign Secretary, and Robert Klingberg, who handled the finances, followed later by Rufus Jones and Fay Richardson.

The task ahead was huge; they had to develop financial and general administrative policies, hire secretarial help, and secure office machines and furniture. This was made difficult by the fact that the war had reached its peak in both the Pacific and in Europe and many goods were in short supply. There were continual comings and goings and countless committees. Ray, in addition to setting up programs, had the task of handling the missionaries who had already volunteered for service, most of whom were veterans, but some of whom were new recruits.

It was not anticipated at that time that the mission would be a large one, and therefore much of the later sophistication in methods and equipment developed as they went along. To begin with, an immense number of tasks waited to be accomplished. Despite his dislike for administrative work, Ray had had valuable experience in Burma where he had been compelled to administer schools, the leprosy colonies, and a number of mission stations, as well as carry out his own work. He had a good knowledge of what was involved in the administration of his former mission. There were many things he could successfully imitate, especially the procedures at home, and there were other areas, especially on the field, where he felt improvements could be made. He was better equipped than most people realized.

The board of the CBFMS was inexperienced at times in missionary work overseas and was almost naive. They tended to think that it was possible to stick pins in a map and begin work in almost any geographic area. They had no idea of the importance of comity arrangements whereby various missions agreed not to overlap and compete with other missions. This and many other fine points had to be explained carefully and patiently. Sometimes missions that were impoverished would ask the CBFMS to take over their work. This took place in India, the Congo, and Argentina, among other places. The CBFMS was still a baby mission and there were limits as to what they could undertake at times for it seemed as though they had been born full-grown. Ray had to help set priorities. He also had to warn about the danger of entering into too many fields too quickly, which would result in the mission being spread too thin to be effective.

In 1945 the National Association of Evangelicals (NAE) was formed, with the Evangelical Foreign Missions Association (EFMA) as its missionary arm, and from the beginning Ray played an active role in its program. It soon became influential in many ways such as in mission cooperation, representing evangelical missions to the State Department and the acquiring of visas for missionaries, as well as countless other matters. CBFMS shared in any comity arrangements recommended by the EFMA. This cooperation between the CBFMS and the EFMA has continued to this day, the President of the EFMA for 1981–1983 being Dr. Warren Webster, the General Director of the CBFMS.

Vincent Brushwyler, as a successful pastor of a large church, had also had administrative experience of a different kind and had tremendous driving power. Both he and Ray threw themselves into the work with all their energy, and although the demands on them were very extensive, they did an astonishingly good piece of work.

There was, of course, much to do by way of administration, for new policies had to be developed in relation to the CBFMS supporting churches in the United States. A sound financial structure had to be created, as well as detailed policies regarding matters on the field. In addition to this work in Chicago, all under pressure of time, there were the insistent demands that the mission be represented in churches throughout the country. The work was to be presented as vital and viable so that new recruits would be attracted, with adequate money to support them.

Many of these demands came from American Baptist churches and they were genuinely puzzled by what had taken place. They wanted to know why a new missionary society had been founded, and what it was doing. Having been so closely identified with the American Baptist Convention as a veteran missionary, and having received his doctorate from one of their leading seminaries, Ray was in a unique position to explain with skill and authority why the new mission was needed. The challenge for Ray was great, but it was rewarding to him to see the supplies of money and the number of recruits increasing.

There was one immediate change from the procedures of the American Baptist Foreign Mission Society. Their policy had been that the missionaries' support was to be impersonal. That is, the churches were notified what the annual total budget for the mission was and each church contributed to the missionary society. The society then paid the expenses and salaries of the missionaries. In the Conservative Baptist Foreign Mission Society it was decided from the beginning that they should adopt personal giving as distinct from impersonal. That is, each missionary was required to raise a base of financial support before he or she ever left for the field. There were several advantages in this method. First, the missionaries could be sure that their expenses would be adequately taken care of as they were not permitted to depart for the field until their entire support was pledged. Second, this interest in individuals with the personalized support meant far more prayer support for them in their ministry. Those who gave for personalized support would automatically pray for that missionary. Third, the home churches no longer felt that the mission was an impersonal machine, but they had a vested interest in the personal well-being, both material and spiritual, of the missionaries they sponsored. This was to be a continuing and important feature in the work of CBFMS.

In the beginning, much attention had to be paid to public relations, and the missionaries who volunteered were used extensively in speaking in churches, in making known the needs of the mission work in general, and in their own field in particular. For the larger churches, Vincent Brushwyler and Ray Buker took the principal role in this deputation outreach. They were able to accomplish both aspects of this work because this promotion was supplemented by the missionary appointees' zealous presentation of their work.

It fell naturally into Ray's province as Foreign Secretary to recommend to the CBFMS board suitable procedures for both the mission field and for the acceptance of new recruits. On his advice, the mission adopted the policy of requiring from their male missionaries at least seven years of study beyond high school, and in the case of women six years. This seemed unusual since Allyn and Leila Cooke had received only a Bible college education and J. O. Frazer had had no formal theological training. Ray had learned so much from them and continued to state how much he owed to them, so it seemed to be inconsistent to demand far more education of his new recruits than Frazer and the Cookes had had. Ray had obviously given much thought to this and he could explain his decision. He felt the Cookes were remarkable for the work they accomplished and he reemphasized how much he owed to them, especially during his first term of service. He also explained to the board that missionaries with a lower standard of training lacked a certain breadth and depth in education that limited their ability to mix among any class of people without a sense of inferiority. The British civil service personnel, a very cultured group of people, definitely tended to look down on missionaries who were, although ardent propagators of the faith, substandard in education. It always came as a real surprise that the average Baptist missionary in Burma had two or three more years of training than the average appointee of the Indian Civil Service (ICS).

Ray regarded Frazer in a different light altogether. He knew that he had had an excellent university education in Britain, as well as a wide experience of European travel. He had had a cultured home life and was an accomplished musician. He was in every sense a cultured European gentleman. This meant that he could be at ease not merely with the simple tribesmen of China, but also with high government officials. In addition to this, he had pursued theological studies on his own and had a good knowledge of Chinese and Lisu. Indeed, it was he who had done the pioneer work and the Cookes continued in the pattern he had set.

Ray was seeking for missionaries who were mature and well-educated. The more education they had, the more potential they would have, and he hoped that they would display more creativity. This fact does not always accompany a good education, but it should at least lead to a good foundation. For Ray, graduation from college and seminary had never been a termination in education but only a launching pad for a continuing process of learning by formal and private studies that still continues today. In addition to this formal education, Ray insisted on required reading on the part of all missionary personnel. In the early days, the best books available were *Behind the Ranges,* by Mrs. Howard Taylor, which is the biography of J. O. Frazer, published in 1938, and the two volumes that had been such an encouragement to Ray on the mission field written by Roland Allen, *Missionary Methods: St. Paul's or Ours?* and *The Spontaneous Expansion of the Church and the Causes Which Hinder It.* Still another book was Alexander Hay's *New Testament Practices for Church and Missions.* Later there were other books that became available, but those four were enough to start a person thinking, particularly when accompanied by fairly frequent questions and discussion with Ray himself.

When Ray set these rules for required reading he was also continuing his own reading. Dr. Vergil Gerber, a distinguished missionary statesman, wrote of something he remembered about Ray Buker:

> He would read some 50 pages every night before he would go to bed. It didn't matter what those pages were, he simply wanted to read to keep his mind active. Sometimes they were as far removed from missions as the kind of fish in Alaskan waters. But he always made himself read 50 pages every day. In addition, he always spent considerable time every morning in the Greek New Testament and time and time again as I was with him, I would get up in the morning to see him buried in his Greek New Testament study.

In referring to Ray when he was 81 he wrote:

> His grasp of contemporary missions continues to be amazing. He is always reading. He is corresponding with missions and missionaries. He is reading the latest missiological writings. And I doubt whether anybody is as knowledgeable on world missions today as Ray Buker.

Ray's sister Molly says that when he asked his missionaries to be well read, he asked no more than he himself was exemplifying. Many were so inspired by this that they tried in part, at least, to follow his example. This self-discipline affected every phase of his life. When he was in Burma there was no need for him to run or jog because of the physical demands of his work. Twenty-five years after his return to the States he was inspired by the advocates of jogging. At first it was only with much suffering that he took this up, but keeping at it for six months at the age of 67, he jogged a full mile. At the age of 81 he still runs a half mile daily. In addition to all this, each morning he follows a routine of calisthenics.

During the early years with the CBFMS he was steadily and viciously attacked by members of the American Baptist Mission. Vincent Brushwyler had been an open critic of the ABFMS for so many years that everyone expected him to be active in a new mission, which was in a sense a protest movement. But Ray had been associated with that mission for sixteen years and was extremely valuable to them. Because he had never indulged in unnecessary controversy he was the one they singled out for their attacks. It seems unreasonable, and yet it is to be supposed that in a sense the missionaries felt almost betrayed although he had never hidden the fact that he disagreed with them on many points. Again and again in his life his soft voice and easy manner led people to underestimate the fact that he had beliefs that were deeply held and for which he would fight with a dogged courage.

Soon the public ministry of Vincent Brushwyler and Ray Buker, coupled with the testimony of the high caliber of the new missionaries, began to have its impact on local churches. Some of these had been withholding funds from the American Baptist Foreign Mission Society because they were so out of sympathy with its theological position. Now they eagerly awoke to the new possibilities that were presented by the Conservative Baptist Foreign Mission Society. The trickle of recruits and funds rapidly became a stream.

Most mission boards hold candidate schools for a period of three to four weeks when the missionary is oriented into the policies of the mission, and in turn is subjected to intense observation on the part of mission leaders. Some of the board felt that the Conservative Baptists should have such a school, but Ray was opposed to the idea. He was convinced that only actual experience on the field would show the ability of a missionary to cope with culture shock, language learning, and interpersonal relationships with fellow missionaries and nationals alike. Further education would also continue constantly through books, continuous correspondence, and interviews. Ray did hold three days' orientation with all recruits and it was followed up by extensive correspondence and visits to them on the field.

So the months sped by and the first year of the history of the mission saw advance along all fronts. By September 2, 1945, when the Japanese signed the document of surrender, an enormous amount of progress had been made and the new mission began to develop on a sound foundation.

The Conservative Baptist Foreign Mission Society was an American mission, and yet it is interesting that included among the first batch of recruits the new mission sent to the mission field was a group of veteran British missionaries.

It is important to understand a little of the background of British missionary societies and the effect that World War II had on the missionary outlook worldwide. One small mission that worked in India, the Korku and Central India Hill Mission (KCIHM), had suffered during the war from erosion of both its missionary personnel and funds from Britain. What this mission went through is simply a microcosm of what happened to almost every British missionary society during the war. Throughout the world a few British missionaries had volunteered for the military; many more who worked in territories occupied by the Italians or the Germans were captured or put under house arrest; shipping was almost nonexistent for missionary personnel, strict financial controls were made by the Bank of England to safeguard its rapidly diminishing coffers, and of course no new missionaries of military age were able to go to the mission field. It is of interest to note that in Britain women were drafted into the armed services as well as men, and the number of people per capita recruited into the armed services, both men and women, exceeded that of any other country in the world, including Russia and Germany. Naturally, the repercussions on the missionary picture were enormous.

Norman Grubb, in a missionary article, stated that just as world leadership during the war had passed from Britain to the United States, so it would be true of missionary work after the war. Before World War II approximately two-thirds of the missionaries in the world came from Britain and one-third came from the United States, but after the war this situation was completely reversed. Therefore the British missions almost invariably had to turn to the United States because Great Britain was in a serious condition both economically and spiritually, and the spiritual situation has deteriorated to the present day.

So, two of the few remaining missionaries of the Korku and Central India Hill Mission (KCIHM) came to the United States to seek some financial help and they were told about the formation of the new American mission, the Conservative Baptist Foreign Mission Society. The first reaction was one of suspicion because the only Baptist mission they had known was the Baptist Missionary Society of Great Britain, which was dominated largely by people who were theologically liberal. But they changed their minds when they were shown the doctrinal statement of the new mission and also a copy of the constitution of CBFMS. On the basis of this, negotiations continued and in September 1945 a tentative merger between the two missions was signed. It was then decided that Ray Buker as the Foreign Secretary should conduct an "on the spot" survey of the mission in India as to its properties and its personnel. This was to be his first overseas journey as Foreign Secretary of the new mission and it lasted from December 1945 until March of 1946.

Although the war was over, almost all shipping was needed to bring troops home from overseas. But Ray eventually was able to obtain passage on a ship that left the States in December and it eventually made its way through the Mediterranean, the Suez Canal, and to India. By the time Ray reached the area of missionary work there was only a handful of missionaries left, but he examined these people and also the new CBFMS missionaries who had arrived in India a few months before him. Several of them were veterans, like Dr. and Mrs. Eric Frykenberg, who had been missionaries in India with the American Baptists, and some were new recruits.

While he was in India, word arrived from the British headquarters of the KCIHM that no more money could be sent from Britain to support the missionaries. Ray held extensive negotiations with the missionaries and meticulously examined the actual mission field and the various properties that were on it. In his report he said:

> The field is roughly the shape of a triangle, 135 miles at its base. The area is estimated at 8,000 square miles, a jungle section with hills and valleys, woods and plains, undeveloped for Christianity. It is a great challenge with at least a million souls unclaimed for Christ.

Since the mission field involved five language groups, the new missionary recruits spent many hours at language study. A personality clash developed between one veteran British missionary and one veteran American missionary, but Ray soon discovered the reason for this problem. Both were suffering from a hearing impairment, and each was too busy trying to explain what he believed and was unable to hear what the other party was saying. This had its humorous side, but a solution was readily found when the veteran American missionary elected to work in another area in South India.

Ray traveled by train in India on this visit, and while his survey of the field took quite a bit of time, post-war travel restrictions made things more difficult. He also began a policy that became a standard practice whenever he visited a mission field. He would interview the missionaries individually, and they would have the opportunity of sharing with him in complete confidence their hopes, their fears, their difficulties, and any other problems they wished to discuss. He would, in turn, inquire of them concerning each phase of their work and study, etc., making some useful suggestions. This not only gave the missionaries a sense that they were being looked after, but the interviews provided a solid basis for correspondence in depth that Ray kept up with every missionary on the field.

After he completed his survey he planned to return to the States. However, he had to wait for a ship, and during this time he developed hepatitis. Later he realized there was a purpose in this experience for he was able to sympathize with and help others who suffered from this common "missionary illness." He eventually recovered in time to obtain passage on a ship bound for the west coast of America. Although he had done much traveling during his life, this was actually his first around-the-world trip. He returned to his office and reported to Vincent Brushwyler and the board what he had discovered, and as a result a merger was finalized. When the KCIHM and also the Khirkia Gospel Mission handed over all their property to the CBFMS at least eight beachheads were established from which a continuing work could be promoted in India.

Ray, Jr. had entered Wheaton as a freshman in 1945 and, following the example of his father, was active in cross-country and track events becoming captain of the Wheaton team. He was coached by Gil Dodds, the distinguished American mile runner at that time. Ray, Jr. entered a number of meets running the mile for three years.

By September 1946 the CBFMS had progressed to the point where Dr. Roy Watson and Dr. F. Carl Truex were appointed as area representatives for missionary deputation and pastoral counseling. The mission was growing much faster than had been anticipated in the beginning.

No Association had yet been organized for it was hoped that the CBFMS could still function within the American Baptists, but circumstances reached the point where they were virtually voted out of the American Baptist Convention in September 1946. The new group, the Conservative Baptist Association, was eventually organized during a process that culminated in February 1947. It was a unique and won-- derful event but was not completed without much heartache and constant negotiation, and sometimes bitter wrangling.

The early days of the mission made great demands on all the people who were connected with it. For Ray there were innumerable conferences, an annual overseas tour, reports to be made to the home bases of the mission, and new missionary recruits to be processed. A tremendous amount of representation was required in the churches to acquaint them with the vast opportunities and needs of the new mission. For instance, in the first eleven months of 1945, Ray spoke 374 times in churches throughout the country and addressed some 30,000 people about the needs of the mission. Vincent Brushwyler was likewise occupied, and the supporting churches, as well as the mission, eagerly responded to the tremendous opportunities that were opening for the future. In many respects it would seem as if the CBFMS was established at the worst of times, during all the chaos of a nation at war, but it was also created at a time when it would be ready for tremendous expansion following the war.

During the war years, few if any missionaries were forth-coming from Britain, but many men stationed overseas in the armed services became acquainted with the tremendous needs of missionary work. They returned home with the conviction that they should play a role in world evangelization. Thus, for at least 10 years after the war there was rapid growth in the missionary movement from the United States. The CBFMS benefited greatly not merely from the contribution made by the leaders, but also from the quality of the recruits that began to come in ever-increasing numbers. In 10 years 300 missionaries were sent to the field and 16 new mission fields were opened. Many referred to this as the miracle society because of its rapid growth, historically the most rapid growth of any society in that given period of time. But there was much more to the mission than statistics.

Partly through Ray Buker's tireless efforts from the beginning, the work of the mission began with the most advanced methods of church planting and indigenous methods. As appropriate new books became available, they were also made required reading for the appointees. In 1947 a new book was published entitled *The New Testament Order for Church and Missionary,* by Alexander Hay. The book was radical and at times the exegesis of Scripture might be questioned, but Ray said when questioned about the book, "Ah, but it stimulates thinking! I am determined that we should have missionaries who think and this was one of the books that accomplished this." He also urged his missionaries to read the seven-volume work of Kenneth Scott Latourette, *A History of the Expansion of Christianity,* a massive and definitive history of the missionary outreach of the church from the days of the New Testament. Ray in his enthusiasm for this set of books promoted the sale of more than two hundred sets. Missionaries who read this finest of historical records of missions reflect the fact in the maturity shown in their approach to missions. To again quote Dr. Vergil Gerber:

One of the things I remember most about Ray was his instilling in me the idea of disciplining my life. He rarely visited me on the field or saw me in the States but what he would ask me "have you read Latourette yet?" and finally in Costa Rica I determined I would read the seven volumes completely through before I saw him again. And I did.

In 1946 the mission undertook work in China, and sent seventeen missionaries. These were eventually forced out in 1952 by the Communist takeover. In 1945 the mission entered Portugal. The next year they began work in Argentina and in the Northeast section of Brazil. Many of these developments were going on concurrently. The field in Zaire, then known as Belgian Congo, was taken over by the CBFMS this same year, 1946.

The work load for Ray increased for he found it necessary to visit two continents each year and he continued his policy of conferring with each of the missionaries. He was also a patient listener during his counseling sessions. Although these visits accomplished much, they above all gave a solid background for future correspondence. Another unusual policy he instituted was that any missionary on the field was free to write to Ray knowing that what he or she wrote would be kept in strict confidence. The general Christian public sometimes fails to realize that the missionary is human and often needs pastoral encouragement and counseling. Missionaries are subject to every problem faced by the Christian at home, plus many more. They may struggle with language problems, culture shock, personality friction with both local Christians and missionary colleagues. Satan uses all these things to try to discourage the missionary. Ray was the ideal person to deal with these problems for he could talk and write with great sympathy and understanding, which was developed only by having passed through those struggles himself.

Although at this point we are mainly concerned with Ray

and the work overseas, it should not be overlooked that the home policies of the mission were extremely sophisticated and advanced. In fact, the home administration of the Conservative Baptists is one of the best in North America.

All missionaries were expected to raise their own support. However once the missionary reached the field, his personal allowance was guaranteed. While the missionaries were by no means affluent, their financial needs were adequately taken care of. The same was true when they returned on furlough, as they were granted a furlough allowance. As with most missions, the missionaries were given a thorough physical examination and all medical needs were met. In due time missionaries on furlough were encouraged to take further education. A number of these went on eventually to obtain doctorates in various fields related to missionary studies and work. In 1950 the denomination established a seminary at Denver, Colorado. In 1951 Dr. Carey Thomas became the first president and Dr. Vernon Grounds became the dean. In 1956 Dr. Thomas died and Dr. Grounds became the president.

By this time the work was expanding rapidly and there were fields that had to be surveyed and visited annually. In 1952, when missionaries were forced out of China, Ray surveyed the Philippines and Taiwan, and as a result missionary work was begun in each of these countries. His insistence on the finest education possible for his missionaries at times led him to encourage them to take unusual steps. His own son undertook two assignments as a pastor of local churches, and when he and three other appointees were compelled to wait for Pakistan visas after their applications for India visas had been turned down, Ray encouraged them to attend the Kennedy School of Missions at Hartford Seminary in Connecticut. At that time it was the only school of missions in the country, but it was very liberal in its theology. Ray, Sr. judged that both Warren Webster and Ray, Jr. had had a solid enough theological education to be able to be exposed to liberal theology without any danger. Webster reported that the experience he gained by attending the Kennedy School of Missions was invaluable for his future career as a missionary and later as a mission executive. Ray, Jr. and he both went to Pakistan in 1954.

The Board came to the conclusion that for every 200 missionaries that joined the mission they would need one Foreign Secretary, so the need arose and Rev. Milton Baker, a pastor at Dover, New Hampshire, was recommended as another Foreign Secretary.

Milton Baker was regarded by some on the board as too young and inexperienced. He was approximately thirty, had never been a missionary, but had been a member of the CBFMS board since its inception. And he was an enthusiastic missionary pastor. Every time Ray paid a visit to New England Milton Baker would ask him to visit at the Dover parsonage. They would spend hours together while Milton asked him searching questions concerning the board minutes, Ray's foreign trips, and missionary work. Ray regarded him as the best informed and most receptive member of the board.

Eventually he was invited to become the Assistant Foreign Secretary to work with Ray, but at this time his church was growing rapidly so he had to refuse for he was in the middle of a building program. The board then asked Ray what they should do. Ray replied that if he was in love with a girl and they could not get married at once he would wait for her. The Board investigated several possible candidates without any results, finally waiting until Milton Baker was free. He was appointed in 1952 and became responsible for the CBFMS fields in Africa and South America, while Ray was held responsible for the whole of Asia and Europe.

Milton was soft-spoken, very friendly, and always cooperative on any missionary committee. He was an effective peacemaker, but could rise to great emergencies as was necessary during the ugly fighting that ensued after freedom had been given to the Belgian Congo and several missionaries were killed. He had to make emergency trips to the area to consult in the evacuation of the missionaries of the CBFMS.

During these early years of the mission and the denomination, there continued to be much unrest. This was caused not only by the American Baptists but also by people within the ranks of the Conservative Baptist Association who wished for a much harder line on various matters of theology and, in particular, on eschatology.

The association held a premillennial view of the return of Jesus Christ but some wished for them also to hold a pre-tribulation view, which was greatly resisted. There were times in the annual meetings of the Conservative Baptist Association in the mid-50s when feelings would become very bitter as this subject was debated. The people who wished for these and other changes were referred to as the hard liners, or sometimes the hard shell. Eventually, these people either took a more tolerant view or, in a few cases, left and joined other groups, but it did not produce an easy climate in which to work.

Ray had some interesting personal habits that were reflections of his own personality. One missionary reported that often when it was time for coffee break in the mission headquarters Ray Buker would be hovering around and would engage a missionary in conversation. Eventually the missionary, knowing that Ray never drank coffee, wondered if there was any significance in this and discovered that there was. Rather than summon a missionary into his office for an interview, whenever possible Ray would seek to put it on a much more informal basis by conducting a conversation during the coffee break. At no time did he attempt to intimidate missionaries.

The board also introduced a practice from the beginning that whenever an officer of the Society traveled overseas he would take at least one pastor with him. They realized from former experiences with the American Baptists that it was of vital importance that the pastors at home, especially those who were influential in the association, should be able to see the mission work and understand the reason for each policy. With Ray at their side, they were carefully briefed on the basic methods and principles of indigenous missionary work, and thus they would be in a much better position to counsel during the Board meetings.

During all these years his twin, Dick, had remained at home because of a deeply held conviction that he and his wife were responsible for the care of her aged and infirm parents. By 1952 this responsibility had been fulfilled, so he wrote to the American Baptists and also to the Leprosy Mission and offered his services.

The American Baptists replied by return mail saying that in view of the critical attitude Dick had displayed toward the American Baptists, they were surprised at his impertinence at suggesting that he resume working with them. He also received a letter from the Leprosy Mission informing him that they would be delighted to make use of his skilled services in Thailand. A few days later the American Baptists, having given more thought to the matter, changed their minds and wrote saying they would be glad to have Dick work with them. Eventually an arrangement was worked out whereby he went out as an American Baptist on loan to the Leprosy Mission for work in the Presbyterian mission in northern Thailand.

Dick would like to have gone out with the CBFMS, but that was impractical, because the CBFMS had no medical work in the area of his linguistic ability. Thus it was he went to Thailand, where his special skills were much needed.

Since Ray and Dick were identical twins there were many opportunities to fool people. In Chicago Dick once stayed with Ray for a few days and Ray suggested that they try an experiment. Dick would go to Ray's office and pass himself off as Ray. Their appearance is identical, and each knew much of the thought processes of the other twin. Dick had so much knowledge about missionary work that he sat in Ray's office for a whole morning interviewing missionaries and other personnel, and gave them the advice he knew Ray would give. When lunch time came, Ray's secretary came into his office and said, "Dr. Buker, I have no doubt that you are Dr. Buker, but I do have some doubt that you are *our* Dr. Buker." She was the only person that morning who had seen through the impersonation, and it even took some time for her to discover it.

Dick then went on to Thailand and performed a marvelous missionary service for many years among leprosy victims in that country.

The demands of the mission with the extensive deputation work, administration, foreign travel, meetings of missionary executives, etc., would have been more than enough to fully occupy the time of any one man, but Ray still persisted in reading his 50 pages every day, and still persisted in his studies in Greek. In addition to all that, he had a great heart for young people, so he served on the board of the Overseas Christian Servicemen's ministry, which maintained canteens and clubs for servicemen in many countries of the world, including the Philippines, Okinawa, Japan, Spain, among others. Ray also served on other boards, including those of the Inter-Varsity Christian Fellowship and on their Missionary Committee as well as the board of the American Indian Crusade. The breadth of his activities indicates the scope of his interests.

The Conservative Baptist Home Mission Society was founded in 1949 with Dr. Rufus Jones becoming its first General Director in 1952. One unusual policy was that the Central American countries were the province of the Home Mission rather than the Foreign Mission. This was a carry over from the policy of the American Baptists.

In 1955 Ray went on another extensive trip around the world. This time it was with four prominent CBFMS officials:

Dr. George Thompson, Dr. Woodrow Rood, Dr. Vance Webster, pastor of the First Baptist Church in Eugene, Oregon, all of whom were pastors and members of the board of the CBFMS, and Walter Fricke, a member of the headquarters staff of the mission. This trip became known as the "Trip of the Big Five."

They visited eight fields of the CBFMS including Pakistan where Warren Webster, the son of Dr. Vance Webster, and Ray Buker, Jr. shared one home with two other new missionary families. For Ray it was a moving experience to see his only child working as a missionary, and he was particularly impressed by the fact that although the four families were crowded in such primitive conditions there was no friction. He knew how easily such an arrangement could lead to a bad situation. The tour was a long one, but it was part of the process of keeping the board members well informed of the field situation and gave them an opportunity to see firsthand how the missionary methods were being put into practice. This was also the last tour for Ray as the Foreign Secretary of CBFMS.

From the time it opened in 1951 the Conservative Baptist Theological Seminary at Denver had been requesting Ray to join the faculty as Professor of Missions. His foreign trips took him away from home two to four months. Speaking tours in the States kept him away from home a third of the time. Dorothy's health by this time prevented her traveling with him. This led him to accept the post of Professor of Missions in the seminary at Denver in 1956. His place as Foreign Secretary was taken by a CBFMS missionary to Italy, Edwin Jacques. During the eleven years he served as the Foreign Secretary, Ray had laid an excellent foundation for future growth of the mission.

For a man who hated administration and never had any ambition for authority, he had performed a solid piece of work. Those years constituted one of the more distinguished periods of his life. He had seen more than 300 missionaries appointed and proceed to the field. He had supervised them, trained them, and under his leadership they had entered sixteen different countries. By the time he resigned from his position, the work was being placed in the hands of the local Christians in most of these countries. The relationship between missionaries and nationals was one of fellowship and brotherhood rather than of boss and servant. He had found his work as Foreign Secretary satisfying, and he knew that it was the will of God. Despite that, at the end of eleven years of very satisfying service he felt that he would rather have been a missionary on the field—in the front lines as it were.

The lessons learned during his service in Burma were never forgotten but they were applied effectively on the worldwide scene. Thus it was that he was indirectly responsible for the salvation of thousands of people throughout the world.

# 11

# PROFESSOR OF MISSIONS

In 1956 Ray began his duties as Professor of Missions at the Conservative Baptist Theological Seminary (CBTS) in Denver, at the age of 57. Those who judge his life on the basis of the following eleven years are doing so on what was probably the least distinguished part of his outstanding life. That is not to suggest that he was by any means a failure, rather that his accomplishments before and after that period were not matched by his work at the seminary.

Denver Seminary became the first institution of its kind in the Conservative Baptist Association when it was founded in 1951. A strong missionary emphasis became its central focus in keeping with the challenge for a worldwide outreach that surged through the churches in those early years of the Association. It was noted, however, that not until five years later was it possible to fill the position of Professor of Missions when Ray Buker was appointed.

The interim was filled by a succession of missionaries from their fields, who each served for a period of approximately one year during their furlough. Bill Peck, missionary home from India, was the one who developed the basic mission curriculum.

When Ray went to Denver to become Missions Professor it was envisioned that the school would have an ambitious missionary program that would offer many courses on the graduate levels, ultimately leading to a doctorate. In reality, however, the school at this period had only 100 students. It was struggling financially and was nonaccredited, and the plans being made for such an ambitious program had to be drastically modified.

One distinguished member of the Conservative Baptist Foreign Mission board once said about Ray's teaching, "His courses were unorganized and nonacademic." This man had not been a student of Ray Buker, but he was merely relaying the impressions he had gained from many who had been. When Ray was asked to evaluate his own performance he replied with characteristic modesty, "I was not a professional teacher. Academically, I had no earned doctorate."

This judgment needs to be put in true perspective. In 1956 it was not particularly fashionable to be interested in missionary work. Today there are a number of graduate level institutions where the science of missions offered on a graduate level has received great respectability and doctorates are no longer uncommon. For years it was true that in every major evangelical seminary in the United States the Professor of Missions was regarded as the lowest man on the totem pole.

Ray knew that missionary work provided a rich variety of challenges to be faced, such as language training, cross-cultural communication, linguistics, and other technical fields as well. He realized that such training should appeal to the intellect and the will, as well as to the emotions, which he felt had a vital part in a spiritual call to carry the gospel around the world. To this end he sought to fashion his teaching to accomplish these goals.

The 1950s were somewhat in contrast to the immediate postwar period when many men had returned from various foreign countries from military service and as a result received a call to the mission field. By 1957 this reservoir of manpower was being integrated into the educational phase of missionary preparation. This, as we have seen, accounted in part for the remarkable growth of the CBFMS, but by the end of the 1950s the postwar surge had begun to plateau. During the first ten years of the seminary nearly 50 percent of the graduates chose the career of missions.

It will be helpful to summarize the handicaps under which Ray undertook this work and to itemize the advantages that were on his side.

### The Handicaps

First, there was the general climate that we referred to above. Second, Ray was described as being unorganized and unacademic. Third, he physically lacked "presence," or to use the term that was not then in vogue, "charisma." Fourth, he was in a small institution of some 100 students, and his classes were small, rarely exceeding 30 in number. Fifth, by nature he was nonassertive and was not a forceful speaker.

### The Advantages

First, to describe his work as being nonacademic is misleading. Very few people know how distinguished his academic record was at every stage of his life. Few, if anyone outside of his family, knew how close he had been to achieving his Phi Beta Kappa in college. Second, few people knew that as far back as 1943 he had been invited to join the faculty of the Eastern Baptist Seminary in Philadelphia, an invitation that would not have been issued had he not been considered to be adequate by that well-established and highly regarded theological seminary. Third, he had eight years' study of Greek, as well as the study of Greek history and philosophy. This was followed by intense practical use of New Testament Greek in translation work in Burma and also in his own personal devotions, but Ray was always totally disinterested in his status.

Fourth, most professors of missions were men who had

served in one mission field, such as China or India, but Ray came from a background as Foreign Secretary where he had studied the entire world, and was able to bring a world-wide perspective to his teaching.

For a period of more than ten years, beginning in 1958, Ray spent about five weeks each summer at a missionary camp in the Upper Peninsula of Michigan, not far from Sault Ste. Marie. He would speak there about most phases of missionary work. It should be explained that although this camp held less than 100 students at a time, it was a very unusual camp in that it was made up mainly of university graduate students, and it had a very distinguished faculty. The other lecturers who participated year by year included the following: Arthur Glasser, Clyde Taylor, Kenneth Strachan, Eugene Nida, William Smalley, David Howard, Waldron Scott, Oswald Sanders, Robert Foster, Phil Armstrong, Dayton Roberts, and David Adeney. The only speakers who were there annually were Ray Buker and Arthur Glasser. On one occasion Dr. Oswald Sanders, the General Director of the Overseas Missionary Fellowship, wrote to Arthur Glasser, who was the North American Director for that mission, and asked him why he felt it worth his while to spend two weeks each summer lecturing to such a small group of students. Glasser's reply was to the effect that he attended because of what he learned as well as what he taught. Dr. Sanders later attended the camp and was very impressed. It should also be mentioned that the program at the camp was considered to be academically adequate for two seminaries in North America to give credits to their students who attended. For these special students Ray Buker gave an examination at the end of the camp and graded the papers, with a report going to the dean of his seminary. The average camper, however, attended to gain training in evangelism and in the many phases of missionary work.

Ray came back to the camp year after year and was one of the few who stayed an entire month. Some conclusions can be drawn from those summers teaching at the camp. First, his appearance of disorganization. He really wasn't disorganized, but rather he seemed to be handicapped by too much knowledge. He dealt with every subject in such minute detail that he could be boring when in fact he was a mine of information. He did not have too little knowledge but too much. Second, he was not a gripping speaker. He was very good with small groups but not very good in lecturing to a large number. Third, he had tremendous versatility. He could lecture on Islam, Buddhism, world survey, missionary methods, anthropology, or whatever he judged to be the need. He always had approximately ten neat, loose-leaf notebooks that contained his entire series of lecture notes used for his seminary classes. Thus he was able to deal with any subject he was asked to consider. Fourth, he inspired great affection. His interest in individuals and his warm humaneness made him invaluable to the program at the camp.

A problem remained as how to make the most use of his knowledge and his gifts. It was found that the best way to make his vast information available was to hold a forum each morning. The forum, composed of the lecturers and resource people, was set up, using written questions to stimulate and air differing viewpoints. Ray gloried in this format and made available to the students a tremendous range of data that they would not have received in formal lectures. He constantly emphasized the importance of history and especially the importance of disciplined reading. He set the example himself by rarely being seen without a book in his hand.

Quite apart from these relatively academic contributions to the camp there were other dividends because of his presence. We spoke earlier about his knowledge of the stars, and he used to give talks on the stars and their formations regularly after lectures in the evening. Being at the camp placed a person in a unique location to study the constellations visible at that time of the year. By the end of the month interested students could identify all the constellations visible in July and August, such as the northern lights or the Aurora borealis. One year a particular satellite reflected the light even though the observers were in darkness. Ray knew the exact time it would appear and in what part of the sky, and they would watch this phenomenon night after night.

Ray had always been an early riser. Early each morning he would start a campfire on the beach and occasionally a small group of students would join him to discuss anything on their minds. He was so natural and friendly that the age difference melted away and there was no generation gap. His genial nature found expression in every aspect of camp life. He tremendously valued each person as an individual and wanted nothing more than to spend time with them. One of the ways in which he could accomplish this was by giving haircuts. If a student was married he would encourage his wife to come along and learn how to cut her husband's hair. He would then say, "Well, I managed to get forty minutes' talk with four people this afternoon." All said with a little chuckle.

Dorothy was a quiet, gentle lady with white hair and a perpetual smile, and was also a big help at camp. She was an expert on identifying wild flowers and would lead nature walks through the woods for groups of interested people. These people not merely learned much about nature but also came to know and love Dorothy herself.

At seminary, Ray always had a tremendous interest in his students and would go to immense trouble to encourage them. Because he was such a firm believer in graduate level training he did not feel he had an obligation to lecture on anything that his students could obtain from reading. So he constantly urged them to read every new book available. In 1953 a book called *On the Mission Field, the Indigenous Church,* by Melvin L. Hodges, was published. This immediately became required reading for his missions majors at seminary. In 1955 a book by Donald McGavran, *The*

*Bridges of God,* was released and the following year that book became required reading at the seminary.

Ray devised a program whereby each year his classes were able to give particular emphasis to one particular subject, one religion, or one area of the world; in the selection he allowed the subject to be determined by the students. One of his former students has written as follows: "Because Dr. Buker was interested in his students and interested in seeing them succeed, not only in the classroom, but in the life work to which God had called them, he personalized the course of study that we had. For instance, he arranged specific courses for me in the field of American Indian Studies, because he knew that I was planning to be a missionary among American Indians. After I had graduated from seminary his interest in what my wife and I were doing continued.

"We recommended that he be appointed to the Board of Directors of the American Indian Crusade in the early 1960's. He was appointed, and is still serving on that board today. Some of the members of the board have indicated that he has been of greater help to that board than any other individual through the years of its existence." He is still active in this work at the age of 81.

It can be seen from this that Ray was deeply concerned about each of his students and continued for many years to correspond not merely with the missionaries he had seen go to the field but also with his former students. His volume of correspondence is impressive.

A couple in New York State thought much of Ray Buker and they arranged to put at his disposal sums of money to help build a missionary library at the seminary. Warren Webster and Ray, Jr. were both missionaries in Pakistan, so Ray arranged for them to advise him on books for the seminary library on Islamics. Following their advice, he ordered books from bookstores throughout the world and eventually compiled what was probably the most complete library on

Islamics in any evangelical seminary in America at that time.

In the same way he built up an excellent section on the American Indians. It will be remembered that he had written his thesis on the Indians of Maine during his first furlough from the field in Burma. He also built up a fairly strong library on Buddhism.

He refused to give a course on the Bible basis of missions and when asked why, he replied, "I regarded that as a subject for undergraduate level and I was interested in teaching at a graduate level. I felt that this was a subject that should be dealt with either by private reading or be obtained before they came to seminary. I would have given such a course, but the academic pressures were just too great to fit this course into the program."

He asked his students to pray for the CBFMS missionaries on their birthdays. It was merely a device he used to keep the attention of his students on the work of active missionaries, and he would explain a little about the work that missionary was doing on that field at that particular time.

Dr. Kenneth Scott Latourette once was lecturing at the Iliff Methodist Seminary in Denver, and because he thought so highly of Ray Buker he insisted on visiting "his friends at the Conservative Baptist Seminary." Ray heard only that morning that Dr. Latourette would be visiting in the afternoon so he corralled as many students as were available to hear the great missionary authority and to chat informally concerning missionary matters.

Several students have written of the tremendous impact Ray had on their lives, apart from his lectures. Dr. Vergil Gerber wrote as follows: "Those who went through Denver Seminary and sat under his teaching caught a fire of missions that they would never get anywhere else. No amount of academic training could ever generate the spiritual dynamic of Ray's personal life and his fire of enthusiasm for world missions."

The Rev. Gordon McDonald, pastor of Grace Chapel at Lexington, Massachusetts, wrote in his church magazine:

> Now he comes to visit me, one of his former students. Our conversation is marked with memories of the past, comments on the present, and projections of the future. Both of us know that visiting time is limited, so we pack into the hour the most worthwhile things we can think to say so that when the time ends, we shall part with no regrets.
>
> A part of me, detached from the conversation, jerks from the storage attic of my mind certain memories. The day, for example, when I cut two of his classes, stayed home, and wrote a paper for a special presentation later that night. When I arrived at the school that evening to read the paper, there he was sitting in the front row, his very presence making me feel a bit uncomfortable for having absented myself earlier in the day. The paper was read and given reasonable audience approval. But when everyone had left the room Buker approached and put his hand on my shoulder.
>
> "Gordon, that was a good paper, but it wasn't great."
>
> I'd expected almost any comment but that. Taken off guard, I walked right into the trap when I asked, "Why, sir?"
>
> The answer has stuck with me since the night it came in 1963: "Because you sacrificed your routine priorities to get it done."
>
> No one that I can remember ever talked to me about the nature of routine. Rather, the message that most often got through was one that pointed to the "spectacular," the "unusual" thing in life as the goal most to be pursued. It took Dr. Buker to demonstrate to me that a race won is a series of small, evenly spaced steps run well; not one enormous, lucky leap.
>
> In business person's terms, he was suggesting

that it is better to "nickel-and-dime one's way to a fortune" than lay all one's hopes on one big frantic shot at the stars. And that has made all the difference in my Christian life, my pastoral life, my family life. The most important thing is the routine matter before me. And out of the routine comes lifelong "greatness." Strangely enough, God can be highly glorified by the woman or the man who serves Him by offering the routine on the altar of praise. Seventeen years later I am still struggling to internalize the meaning of that single bit of character-lesson.

Raymond Buker also taught me something about the meaning of discipline. He was known among students for refusing to drink coffee. Did he not like it? Was it unhealthy for him? No, he told me one day, it was merely a matter of turning one's back on certain things in life simply to insure that one had not lost touch with the ability to say *no* to appetites and passions.

His was a lonely voice on such matters. But in the jungles of Burma during the early years of the Japanese occupation when his life and those of his family were on the line, he'd learned the hard way that there come times when one must be hardened and disciplined to face stress and suffering. And, he would add, one does not learn such rigors at the last minute. Rather, one "practices" for such moments. We condition, he often said, in the easy times, in order to perform in the more difficult times.

It was a lonely voice then, and it is a lonely voice today. But he was right. And he taught me the value of selecting something one likes and saying "no" to it for a while, simply to keep well-tuned the ability . . . to say "no."

I really can't remember a whole lot of what my old missions professor said in the classroom. He knows that, and he often used to despair (painfully to my face) that I would probably never amount to much. But what even he failed to realize was that while I might have been a hopeless student of missionary anthropology—languages always were my blindside—I absorbed everything he had to say and do about Christian character. And his lessons both about routine and discipline will live on in my soul until I die.

He's an old man now, retired from teaching but not from traveling the world encouraging younger people to carry on where he has left off. And he sits in my office with a grin on his face. "Gordon," he says, "you amaze me. I never thought you learned anything, and I never thought you'd accomplish anything. Now look at you in this wonderful, large church. I'm so glad."

When he leaves my study after our visit I sit and brood for several minutes. Suddenly I find myself praying, "Lord, help me to be the kind of man that teaches people *character* like Jesus Christ's. That's much better than impressing folks with facts and figures they're sure to forget."

Another student, the Rev. Arthur Everett of International Students, Inc., writes:

> While I was in seminary, many of the students did not like the seeming disorganization of Dr. Buker. They took his courses only because they had to because certain ones were required. Some of these students considered themselves "the intellectual elite" and felt that what he had to offer did not quite come up to their standards. However, I learned so much from the man. He had so much to give for those who would just absorb from him. No he was not as organized as some other professors, but what I learned just from the man, from his experience, from his personality, from everything that surrounded him, was really the highlight of my seminary education.
>
> I did talk with one of those students who complained about Dr. Buker's courses while we were

there. I talked with him about a year after he graduated from Seminary, and he said to me, "If I had it to do over, I'd major in missions, and take all the courses I could under Dr. Buker." He had learned, probably too late, some of what Dr. Buker had to offer.

While I was there in Seminary, Dr. Buker became like a spiritual father to me. He had a keen personal interest in his students. You might say that Dr. Buker was missions personified. He did things that had no relevance to classroom courses. For instance, he taught my wife how to cut my hair, using some of his free Saturday mornings to do this. Why? Because he felt that some day, if I were on the mission field where there were no barbers, she would have to know this. He was practical and what he taught, not only in the classroom, but outside the classroom has been of great practical value in my life since.

Through the years, we have wanted to keep close ties with Dr. Buker. He has counselled and advised me in so many ways and has been the person that I have turned to at especially critical points in my life. On one occasion, someone to whom I looked up a great deal had let me down with a thud by his actions. This man was a Christian leader and I could not understand why he was acting the way he was. Consequently, I made several long-distance calls around the country, before I finally tracked down Dr. Buker. He travelled each summer and it was difficult to contact him. When I did, and when I shared with him my concern, he said to me, "Art, as time goes on, you'll learn that every one of us, you and me included, day after day, by the things we do, rub the name of the Lord in the dirt. But somehow, he still receives glory from it."

This helped me to get my attention off the person involved and the things he had done and to realize also that I was just as guilty in other ways as he.

On another occasion, Dr. Buker gave me a quick answer that helped me to look in the right direction again. I had introduced him to another Christian worker and wanted Dr. Buker to be aware of quirks in this man's personality. So, when I had the opportunity, I simply said to him: "You'll notice that he is a little bit different." Dr. Buker turned to me immediately and said, "Aren't we all?" I appreciated so much his level-headed answers in situations like this that help me to realize that, again, I shouldn't be critical of other people. I should realize that I'm a human being created by God in the same situation as they.

Recently, I called Dr. Buker regarding a present problem. This problem, too, centered around other people. Dr. Buker counselled me by saying: "Don't lay down any ultimatums. Otherwise if things don't happen the way you think they should, you'll be forced to leave with nowhere to go." He knew that I was emotional and not ready to make sound decisions. Again, he proved to be a wise counsellor.

It will be seen from these quotes that not merely his lectures, but his life as well made an indelible impression on many of his students, both at Denver and wherever he went.

His years as Professor of Missions were relatively undramatic compared with much of the rest of his life, but he made a solid contribution to the seminary and to the CBFMS. He counted the students that were serving with the CBFMS and discovered that fifty of his students were serving with that mission, plus a large number with other missions.

He retired from his professorship in 1967 at the age of 67 and was appointed Professor Emeritus of Missions. From time to time, when his successor was compelled to be out of the country or otherwise unavailable, Ray would return to the classroom once more.

The seminary has come a long way since the days when he joined it. It now has an exceptionally attractive and functional campus and is fully accredited. One section of the library has been dedicated as "The Buker Alcove," and this is where his donated private library is housed. The comfortable study chairs and beautiful globe of the world, along with a glass case of artifacts representing life in many lands, adds a quiet charm and reflective setting for every reader.

# 13

# A VIGOROUS
# RETIREMENT

For Ray Buker retirement could never mean a rocking chair. It was rather a period when he could implement the results of all the lessons learned in a fruitful and varied career. God had used his life as a stepping stone to prepare his retirement as a time of ever-increasing influence. It was almost a parallel to the years of his grueling training where every victory had paved the way for higher achievement.

Ray had always been concerned about both the quality and amount of education missionaries received, as well as the educational systems that were established for the nationals. Among the conservative missions, education often extended only to the primary or to high school level, although it was sometimes followed by Bible college.

Among the missionary societies connected with the World Council of Churches, education was much more sophisticated and huge sums of money were available for advanced education in the USA, up to doctoral level. This meant that when conferences took place between national Christians in any given continent those from conservative backgrounds were at a disastrous disadvantage compared with their more liberal countrymen.

The glaring contrast between the two began to arouse much tension in the 1960s, and missionary statesmen felt that some steps should be taken to rectify the situation in evangelical missions. Thus came into being an organization known as the Committee to Assist Ministry Education Overseas (CAMEO). It was composed of twenty missionary leaders and Christian educators, an equal number from each of two outstanding and well-known mission associations: the Evangelical Foreign Missions Association (EFMA) and the Interdenominational Foreign Missions Association (IFMA). Two co-chairmen selected were Dr. Milton Baker, one of the overseas secretaries of Conservative Baptist Foreign Mission Society who represented EFMA, and Dr. Delbert Kuehl, Executive Assistant Director of the Evangelical Alliance Mission (TEAM), representing IFMA. Originally, the plan was to operate without a coordinator, using the co-chairmen for this purpose, but the mission responsibilities for the co-chairmen took them out of the country on frequent trips, causing CAMEO's operation to become ineffective. By 1967 it was decided that a coordinator should be appointed to guide its procedures. This coincided with the retirement of Ray Buker from his position as Professor of Missions at the Denver Seminary so he was invited to take the position. It proved to be an excellent appointment.

Dr. Delbert Kuehl writes as follows:

> I started with the group that finally brought CAMEO into being from its early beginning and I can say that CAMEO didn't accomplish that which we wanted until Ray Buker, Sr. became the coordinator. Ray served as coordinator until May 1, 1975.

Ray was sixty-eight years old but as alert and creative as ever. He accepted the challenge that the appointment offered, and welcomed the opportunities to broaden its influence. His whole life had been a preparation for it. He probably made a more extensive contribution during this time than in any previous period of his life. Instead of working within one mission his work now brought him in vital contact with almost every group connected with the Evangelical Foreign Missionary Association (EFMA) and the Interdenominational Foreign Mission Association (IFMA). This meant that he was working with virtually every evangelical foreign mission in North America.

Ray was not a trained educator but that was not important, for he was excellent at delegating responsibility to others. He soon discovered that CAMEO was disorganized but trying hard. He inherited five or six committees, but he had been given no job description.

He learned that Dr. Ted Ward in the Systems Learning Institute at Michigan State University had assisted the Far Eastern Gospel Crusade to set up a successful educational program, so he went to him for advice.

Dr. Ward insisted that three steps must be taken. First, a thorough survey needed to be carried out. Second, the information from this survey had to be collated and examined. Third, a program had to be set up to implement the recommendations from the skilled advisors.

The executives of the Liberty Foundation near Philadelphia were willing to invest money in such a creative missionary enterprise, and Ted Ward's recommendations (approved by CAMEO) were accepted by this foundation. He explained to them the great need of this educational program on the mission field and the enormous potential for good that it promised, and they responded by promising a generous gift of a quarter of a million dollars.

Armed with this advice from Dr. Ward and the promise of a quarter of a million dollars from the De Moss brothers, Ray returned to Denver. He then wrote a comprehensive questionnaire and used the seminary students as secretarial help to conduct the survey. From the information gathered in this survey he produced the World Directory of Mission-Related Educational Institutions. The directory accumulated by the computers of Michigan State University ran to 500 pages, took two years to complete, and was published by the William Carey Press.

Soon after the directory was published, following a meeting of the National Association of Evangelicals (NAE) in Philadelphia, Ray arranged for a group of approximately twenty-five knowledgeable people to be gathered together at that time. This group included Peter Wagner, Harold Alexander, Ted Ward, Ralph Winter, Allen Thompson, and other missionary experts.

The conclusion arrived at in this conference was that CAMEO would sponsor a workshop during the period between Christmas and New Year's Day to discuss Theological Education by Extension (TEE). Two foundations gave a total of $9,000 to make this possible. Ray invited all EFMA and IFMA missionaries home on furlough interested in education to this workshop, which was held at Wheaton, Illinois. One hundred and twenty were present; their expenses having been paid from the monies raised by Ray for this purpose. This was the first workshop on TEE to be given in the United States.

Theological Education by Extension (TEE) was first conceived by Presbyterian missionaries in Guatemala. Two or three highly qualified men with graduate degrees were teaching there in a seminary. Over a period of years they realized that the results were not comparable to the input. Men with doctoral degrees taught from twenty to forty students, hoping to prepare these men for Christian service among their own people. To the dismay of the faculty, it was noted that perhaps 50 percent of the graduates were using their Christian training as a stepping stone to remunerative secular jobs. Churches in great need of qualified leadership were hurting. Their young men were not coming back to serve in the local church, owing largely to the fact that they were not properly motivated.

The missionary educators reviewed the situation carefully. The local church leaders were inadequately prepared and recognized their lack, but with families and jobs to supplement the low pastoral remuneration it was impossible for them to move to a distant city and take a year or two of study in the seminary. After consultation together, the educators devised a workable plan whereby opportunities to study would be provided to natural national leaders who economically could not enter a seminary. Centers were selected where four or five or more national workers could gather once a week for a half day. The missionary went to them. Because home study was maximum and class work at a minimum, specially prepared material in the various disciplines of the seminary curriculum called programmed texts were prepared. These programmed texts were autodidactic. The individual could study and learn by himself. Weekly class sessions were used to discuss the application of the subjects to the work in which the national worker was involved.

This new procedure became known as Theological Education by Extension. At the Wheaton Seminar/Workshop this concept was initially presented and augmented by missionaries from two or three countries where the TEE plan was already in use.

There are now more than 55,000 students in 360 programs in 80 countries studying through TEE. Since the last survey was conducted three years ago there has been an increase of 50 percent, and the movement has spread to 20 additional countries. TEE classes are currently being held in some 80 languages. A survey shows Africa with 20,974, surpassing South America with 20,507 as the region reporting the most TEE students.

The first response to this program was enthusiastic. One missionary from Brazil immediately asked for a workshop to be held in his country, and further requests began to come from other countries. Workshops began to be held with the coordination, personnel, text, and books supplied by CAMEO. Ray set up two teams of two men each who became resource men in the area. The first team traveled to Asia, another team traveled to Africa, and in 1969 Ray himself traveled to Africa, France, Senegal, Kenya, and the Ivory Coast. The first year was so successful that the experiment was repeated the second year, and it was between 1970 and 1973 that TEE was launched worldwide.

By 1973 TEE had compiled three invaluable tools: one, the book *TEE Manual for Workshops;* two, a primer by Dr. Peter Wagner and Dr. Ralph Covell, covering a trip around the world where summer overseas courses were set up, which material was still being used in 1980; and three: a book on programming techniques for TEE by Dr. Ted Ward, produced in four languages: English, Portuguese, Spanish, and French. With these manuals and materials TEE became a reality in almost every country in the world. The only two areas which have been slow to adopt it are Japan and Africa.

Through the activity of Marjorie Shelley, director of literature work in the Ivory Coast, material slowly became available in French. One interesting aspect of this is that the program is being applied in French-speaking Montreal, Canada. The work is still going forward through the translation of material prepared by Dr. Fred Holland of Wheaton Graduate School into local languages and dialects. In Africa the first workshops that were held not merely succeeded in recruiting individuals, but from that there sprang the Association of Evangelicals of Africa and Madagascar (AEAM). As the work progressed some thirty programmed textbooks were completed, and all this came as a result of the ministry of CAMEO.

One outstanding example of the work of CAMEO is that undertaken by Lois McKinney. Dr. Ted Ward encouraged her to take her Doctorate at Michigan State University, majoring on the skills needed in TEE. She formulated a plan to train Brazilians to write texts, sponsored by CAMEO. This program lasted one year whereby twenty Brazilian teachers developed writing skills for the programmed texts. Dr.

McKinney succeeded Ray Buker as the director of CAMEO and TEE International, traveling constantly throughout the world, holding workshops that present features relative to CAMEO's purposes.

Marjorie Shelley is still very active in the French work. It is estimated that twenty more books are needed for Africa alone, and each book will take $400 to produce. She is trying to raise $8,000 for twenty books plus another $7,000 for production, a total of $15,000. Once the novelty of TEE began to wear off, foundations who had supplied so much of the money to make it possible became far less willing to offer their help, so money is always in short supply. Since it is no longer forthcoming from foundations, Ray Buker feels that there are two remaining challenges: first is that of developing TEE and applying it to minorities in North America, and second is that of a person who will act as a promoter, particularly in raising money from churches for the ministry of CAMEO.

One notable book has recently been published, *Discipling Through Theological Education by Extension,* edited by Vergil Gerber. The dedication reads as follows:

> To Raymond Buker, Sr., whose tireless efforts on behalf of theological education by extension around the world made his name synonymous with CAMEO (Committee to Assist Ministry Education Overseas), of which he served as coordinator until 1975.

Dr. Delbert Kuehl has paid the following compliment to Ray Buker in a recent letter:

> Ray served as our coordinator for eight years and he still continued to serve as a consulting coordinator. Ray had a real ability to gain the confidence of people. This was with the men who served closely with him on the committee and of groups that he would appeal to regarding the outreach of CAMEO, individuals, and foundations for funds, and the

mission organizations, schools, and so forth that CAMEO was serving. I was always deeply impressed with Ray's humility. He was a man of tremendous knowledge, broad background, good judgment, yet a very humble man. We couldn't have had a finer person to work with national and missionary personnel overseas whom we were trying to assist in the educational outreach. They respected Ray because of his long experience in mission work overseas, then in executive responsibilities in the homeland and teaching a number of years in a seminary classroom.

Ray never left the impression as he contacted overseas personnel of knowing it all and now coming to instruct them, or like a big brother with his hand on the shoulder of a little brother, but as a partner in the work with a real desire to assist. Ray is widely known in mission circles so there are not many who are not aware of his tremendous background of experience. He was received in a most unusual way by overseas personnel and also by groups with whom he was in contact in relationship to CAMEO's outreach here in the States.

I think Ray was used in a marked way in CAMEO also because of his tremendous ability to get along with people. Milton Baker and I greatly appreciated working together with Ray. We served as co-chairmen of CAMEO for a number of years. Ray has real ability to come up with good suggestions, possible programs, but he wasn't resentful if we questioned some areas of his proposals or even suggested changes that we felt should be made, and this was rare, in something he had come up with. On our CAMEO board we had men with years of background in education and missionary work. As I spent many sessions with these men, I could sense without question the tremendous respect they had along with we who were on the Executive Committee for Ray. We can look back and thank this man of

God for really making CAMEO an effective organization in assisting worldwide missionary work, particularly in the field of education. Ray tirelessly
worked on setting up seminars in the U.S. and all
around the world to help missionaries and nationals
particularly, in the Theological Education by Extension program. The success of that program that has
followed in these last years certainly relates to much
that Ray did in the leadership of CAMEO.

Although Ray Buker felt he should make way for a
younger person when he reached the age of 75, he continued
to be active physically and intellectually and still serves as a
consultant for CAMEO at age 81. On his 75th birthday, Ray
celebrated by beating his grandson in a game of tennis! He
asserts that it was a fluke, and that may well be true, but it
says much about a man who was still playing tennis at the
age of 75.

In June of 1977 Dr. Milton Baker died of a heart attack.
This was a grievous loss to CAMEO, and in particular to Ray
Buker, who for thirty years had looked on him as a brother
and a devoted disciple.

In 1969 Ray, Jr. (now Dr. Ray Buker, Jr.) returned from
Pakistan where he had performed remarkable service as a
missionary for more than fifteen years. Refused a visa to
continue work in Pakistan he became the Personnel Secretary for the CBFMS and was responsible for the recruiting of
new candidates.

Dorothy's health had been deteriorating for years, and in
addition to all his other activities Ray insisted on nursing
her personally. He tried to involve her in his activities as
much as she was able, but found she could not take arduous
journeys with him. Although Ray and Dorothy continued to
live in Denver, they found it possible to spend the winters in
Boca Raton, Florida, where Dick carried on his practice in
medicine and where sister Molly provided them a comfortable home. After much suffering Dorothy died on March 19,

1975, terminating a wonderful partnership of fifty-one years.

Even in the earliest years of their marriage Dorothy had known great loneliness brought about by Ray's athletic trips for competition that were part of the price of his successful Olympic career. Following this were the years of heroic service in Burma with its hardships, trials, struggles, and triumphs. Then came the ordeal of the war years, uncomplaining loneliness during the birth of the new Mission, and later as Ray traveled world-wide as Foreign Secretary. Dorothy in her quiet and gentle way was a constant and selfless inspiration in every phase of his life.

Her death was an enormous blow to him, resulting in a depression similar to that experienced in Burma from 1938 to 1942. Friends who met him during that period were alarmed at the deterioration in his condition.

In 1976, after unsuccessful attempts to reconstruct his life, Ray married Mary Margerum, his former secretary in Chicago while he was Foreign Secretary of CBFMS. Later Miss Margerum served with distinction as administrative assistant to four successive presidents at Gordon College and Gordon-Conwell Theological Seminary from 1956 to 1976. In a quaint New England church near the Seminary, Ray and Mary were married June 25, with eight of the Buker clan and a church full of happy friends to witness the joyous occasion.

With many mutual interests Ray soon found life taking on a brighter hue. Outdoor exercises include jogging and swimming which they both find therapeutic and enjoyable.

Ray cherished the desire to take Mary on a trip to the Orient, exposing her to mission fields of the CBFMS, well-known to her, but never before visited, and meeting again missionary friends, dearly beloved by them both. This trip became a reality in the fall of 1978 when for two months, travels to Okinawa, Japan, Hong Kong, the Philippines, Guam, and Hawaii crowded their days with excitement as

Ray saw again the development of work and ministry initiated almost three decades previously. At the age of 79 he found untold satisfaction in the fruit of his labors and in the bountiful blessings of a faithful God.

Moving permanently to Boca Raton, Florida, in 1979 Ray and Mary share in the ministry of their church and in community activities. As chairman of the church's missions committee, Ray gives leadership and counsel born out of years of experience in the world's harvest fields. He is well informed on many facets of missions around the world, shares as a member of the board of the American Indian Crusade, and continues his contacts with the Overseas Christian Servicemen's Centers and with CAMEO.

The CBFMS, as of 1980, has sent 999 missionaries to the field. Of that number 515 are still in active service today, and approximately 400 are in active Christian service. The rest have passed on or are retired. The sixteen fields that were opened when Ray was Foreign Secretary have now increased to twenty-two.

In 1980 he was as active as ever. He was inducted into the Hall of Fame of his preparatory school, Mount Hermon. He traveled to Arizona to fulfill his duties as secretary of the American Indian Crusade, but perhaps most significant of all, he was invited to be a consultant in "Project Lookup," composed of a group of engineers planning to launch a satellite to beam the gospel to remote areas of the world. For a boy who had begun life accompanying his father on preaching engagements on horseback, to being involved in a highly sophisticated project using a satellite was in character for Ray.

Perhaps the final tribute to Ray Buker is best phrased from a letter written by Dr. Vergil Gerber, once a young prodigy of Ray, and now a world-respected missionary-statesman in his own right.

> I doubt if I ever knew a man of God as saintly as Raymond Buker. How many times he brought to me

just the spiritual counsel which I needed or the spiritual correction which was necessary. I shall ever be indebted to him for his contribution to my life.

# EPILOGUE

The theological controversy that caused such a stir among the Presbyterians in 1929 and the American Baptists in 1943 continues to this day virtually throughout the world. Ray Buker is no longer at the center of the storm, but he follows every detail with close interest. In the 1960s and 1970s the controversy spread through the whole of the USA, and in a more subtle way was having its effect in Great Britain.

The controversy built up slowly, but the first major development came in 1973, when after many years of negotiation within the Presbyterian Church US (Southern Presbyterian), conservative leaders voted to leave the denomination and to found the Presbyterian Church of America (PCA). This denomination which started in 1973 with 250 churches, by 1980 had grown to 500 churches with 75,000 members, and 170 missionaries in 23 countries. The PCA includes some of the largest and most influential Presbyterian churches in the south.

In 1976 another significant event was the publication of a book named *The Battle for the Bible* by Dr. Harold Lindsell, and published by Zondervan. The book was a timely one and it dealt in depth with the inerrancy of Scripture. The book covers much ground and gives a survey of the Lutheran

242

Church-Missouri Synod, the Southern Baptist Convention, and also deals thoroughly with the Fuller Theological Seminary.

One of the interesting aspects of the detailed chapter on Fuller seminary is the fact Dr. Lindsell had been on the faculty since the founding of the seminary in 1947 until 1964 when he resigned to become the editor of *Christianity Today.* In this chapter Dr. Lindsell deals at great length with the way in which over a period of years the seminary had begun with a doctrinal statement that believed in the inerrancy of Scripture and how gradually this great erosion took place.

Dr. Lindsell had at one time been dean of the faculty and later a vice president of the seminary, but during the entire period he was the Professor of Missions.

An unrelated but very important event took place in March 1980 when the Tenth Presbyterian Church of Philadelphia resigned from the United Presbyterian Church in the USA (the Northern Presbyterian Church). The pastor at that time was Dr. John M. Boice, who is a very distinguished preacher and theologian. He is the Chairman of the International Council on Biblical Inerrancy and is active in the conferences on Reformed Theology.

The church is a historic one that has had a succession of distinguished ministers, including Dr. Donald Grey Barnhouse. The church leaders had been unhappy with a number of developments in the denomination in recent years, but the issue that led to the ultimate step of severance came in May 1979 when the denomination required that each church had to ordain women elders, regardless of the conscience or convictions of the pastors. The break came only after two years of "prayerful consideration."

The Philadelphia Presbytery requested that Dr. Boice and the elders of the church appear before them, but Dr. Boice indicated that the church had already renounced the jurisdiction of the Presbytery. They had learned from the history of Dr. Gresham Machen. A legal battle is now looming between the church and the Presbytery over the ownership of the property. Tenth Presbyterian Church is 150 years old and for such a famous church to take the great step of severing its connection with the denomination has created a stir throughout the nation. In 1981 the church applied to join the Reformed Presbyterian Evangelical Synod. A number of other Presbyterian churches belonging to the same denomination have resigned from the denomination recently.

The tendency toward theological liberalism seems to accelerate and the tendency for churches to resign from their denominations also continues. For Ray Buker this is sad but he can only look back over a long distinguished life and see that his own experience in leaving the American Baptists was actually a significant incident in theological history.

A war usually consists of a number of battles. The war for biblical conservatism has raged for centuries and will continue to do so until the Lord returns. Ray is an underrated man who, when his time came, did not hesitate to step into the cauldron of theological controversy. In so doing he was behaving as he had throughout his whole life, whether it concerned a minor matter of drinking coffee, his self-discipline in athletics, or missionary methods and theological imperatives. He has always been prepared to stand against the tide, but with Christian courtesy and humor. As such he must surely rank as a rare example of spiritual strength and grace.

Whatever may be the evaluation of man, Ray will surely deserve the greeting of his Lord, "Well done, good and faithful servant." It is the only commendation he has ever sought.

# BIBLIOGRAPHY

In 1974 the British secret archives concerning World War II were declassified. For the first time it was revealed that the British had obtained a copy of a German machine Enigma, which Hitler used to communicate with all his armies. The British exploited this knowledge so well that it helped them to win the Battle of Britain. When messages were sent to Field Marshall Erwin Rommel, Field Marshall Bernard Montgomery often received his copy before his opponent.

Germany made Enigma available to the Japanese and Britain shared this invaluable asset with the USA. This in turn meant that America could and did break the Japanese code, and among many other successes made possible the victory at Midway Island.

No book written before 1974 about World War II was able to reveal the whole truth. The definitive book concerning this is *Bodyguard of Lies* by Anthony Cave Brown. Two other valuable books are paperbacks, *The Ultra Secret* by F. W. Winterbotham, and *A Man Called Intrepid* by William Stevenson.

The same declassification enabled Dusko Popov to write his autobiography *Spy Counter-Spy*. Popov was a Yugoslav who became a priceless double agent working for Britain against Germany. He took enormous risks but gathered invaluable information. There is no indication that he was aware of the tightly controlled secret of Enigma but was able to use the microdot technique. With the highest authority of British intelligence he was sent to the USA in early 1941 to give Edgar Hoover and the FBI indisputable evidence of the impending attack on Pearl Harbor. Hoover had four months notice of the attack but took no action. No satisfactory explanation of this lack of action has ever been published. The whole of the Japanese War in the Pacific would have been changed, if not avoided, and it is conceivable that they could not have attacked Burma.

Allan, Roland. *Missionary Methods: St. Paul's or Ours?* (London: World Dominion Press, 1912).

————. *The Spontaneous Expansion of the Church* (London: World Dominion Press, 1949).

Attlee, Clement. *As It Happened, The Memoirs of a Prime Minister.*

Cauthen, Kenneth. *The Impact of American Religious Liberalism* (New York: Harper & Row, n.d.).

Churchill, Winston S. *The Second World War* (Six Volumes) (Boston: Houghton Mifflin, 1948-53).

Clark, Charles Allen. *The Nevius Plan for Mission Work in Korea* (Seoul, Korea: Christian Literature Society, 1928).

Cleveland, Harlan & Gerard J. Mangone. *The Art of Overseasmanship* (Syracuse: Syracuse University Press, 1957).

Dorn, Frank. *Walkout with Stilwell in Burma* (New York: Thomas Y. Crowell, 1971).

Dunlop, Richard. *Behind Japanese Lines with the OSS in Burma* (New York: Rand McNally, 1979).

Gerber, Vergil (editor). *Discipling Through Theological Education by Extension* (Chicago: Moody Bible Institute, 1980).

Hart, Liddell B. H. *History of the Second World War* (USA: Cassell, 1971).

Hay, Alex R. *The New Testament Order for Church and Missionary* (Audubon, N.J.: New Testament Union, 1947).

Henry, Carl F. H. *Aspects of Christian Social Ethics* (Grand Rapids: Eerdmans, 1980).

Hodges, Melvin L. *On the Mission Field, The Indigenous Church* (Springfield, Mo., Gospel Publishing House, 1953).

Howard, Randolph L. *It Began in Burma* (Chicago: Judson Press, 1942).

Latourette, Kenneth Scott. *A History of the Expansion of Christianity* (Vol. 3) *Three Centuries of Advance A.D. 1500–A.D. 1800* (New York: Harper Bros. 1939).

Lindsell, Harold. *The Battle for the Bible* (Grand Rapids: Zondervan, 1976).

McGavran, Donald. *The Bridges of God* (New York: Friendship Press, 1955).

_____. *How Churches Grow* (London: World Dominion Press, 1959).

Moran, Lord. *Churchill* (Boston: Houghton Mifflin, 1966).

Nicolson, Nigel. *Alex, The Life of Field Marshal Alexander of Tunis* (London: Pan Books, 1973).

Popov, Dusko. *Spy Counter-Spy* (Greenwich, Conn.: Fawcett Publications, 1975).

Rauschenbusch, Walter. *Christianity and the Social Crisis* (New York: Eaton & Mains, n.d.).

Seagrave, Gordon S. *Burma Surgeon* (New York: Norton & Co., 1943).

_____. *Tales of a Waste-Basket Surgeon* (Philadelphia: Judson Press, 1944).

_____. *Waste-Basket Surgery* (Philadelphia: Judson Press, 1930).

Sevareid, Eric. *Not So Wild a Dream* (New York: Knopf, 1946).

Shelley, Bruce L. *A History of Conservative Baptists* (Wheaton: Conservative Baptist Press, 1971).

Stevenson, William. *A Man Called Intrepid* (New York: Ballantine Books, 1979).

Taylor, Mrs. Howard. *Behind the Ranges* (London: Lutterworth Press, 1956).

Tuchman, Barbara W. *Stilwell and the American Experience in China, 1911-1945* (New York: Macmillan, 1970).

Winterbotham, F. W. *The Ultra Secret* (New York: Dell Publishing, 1974).